DEVELOPING CREATIVE
AND CRITICAL
EDUCATIONAL PRACTITIONERS

Critical Guides for
Teacher Educators

You might also like the following books from Critical Publishing.

Developing Outstanding Practice in School-Based Teacher Education
Edited by Kim Jones and Elizabeth White
978-1-909682-41-2
October 2014

Dial M for Mentor: Critical Reflections on Mentoring for Coaches, Educators and Trainers
By Jonathan Gravells and Susan Wallace
978-1-909330-00-9
Published 2012

How do Expert Primary Classteachers Really Work? A Critical Guide for Teachers, Headteachers and Teacher Educators
By Tony Eaude
978-1-909330-01-6
Published 2012

Non-directive Coaching: Attitudes, Approaches and Applications
By Bob Thomson
978-1-909330-57-3
Published 2013

Theories of Professional Learning: A Critical Guide for Teacher Educators
By Carey Philpott
978-1-909682-33-7
October 2014

Most of our titles are also available in a range of electronic formats. To order please go to our website www.criticalpublishing.com or contact our distributor, NBN International, 10 Thornbury Road, Plymouth PL6 7PP, telephone 01752 202301 or email orders@nbninternational.com.

DEVELOPING CREATIVE
AND CRITICAL
EDUCATIONAL PRACTITIONERS

Series Editor: Ian Menter

Critical Guides for
Teacher Educators

Victoria **Door**

First published in 2014 by Critical Publishing Ltd

British Library Cataloguing in Publication Data
A CIP record for this book is available from the British Library

ISBN: 978-1-909682-37-5

This book is also available in the following e-book formats:
MOBI: 978-1-909682-38-2
EPUB: 978-1-909682-39-9
Adobe e-book reader: 978-1-909682-40-5

Cover and text design by Greensplash Limited
Project Management by Out of House Publishing
Typeset by Newgen Knowledge Works
Printed and bound in Great Britain by TJ International

Critical Publishing
152 Chester Road
Northwich
CW8 4AL

www.criticalpublishing.com

MIX
Paper from
responsible sources
FSC   FSC® C013056
www.fsc.org

CONTENTS

FOREWORD

It has become something of a cliché to say that those of us involved in teacher education 'live in interesting times'. However, such has been the rate of change in many aspects of teacher education in many parts of the world over recent years that this does actually need to be recognised. Because of the global interest in the quality of teaching and the recognition that teacher learning and development of teachers plays a crucial part in this, politicians and policymakers have shown increasing interest in the nature of teacher preparation. Early in 2013 the British Educational Research Association (BERA) in collaboration with the Royal Society for the Arts (RSA) established an inquiry into the relationship between research and teacher education. The final report from this inquiry was published in 2014 (BERA/RSA, 2014) and it sets out a range of findings that include a call for all of those involved – policymakers, practitioners, researchers – '*to exercise leadership amongst their members and partners in promoting the use of evidence, enquiry and evaluation to prioritise the role of research and to make time and resources available for research engagement*' (p 27). One key purpose of this series of *Critical Guides for Teacher Educators* is to provide a resource that will facilitate a concerted move in this direction. The series aims to offer insights for all those with responsibilities in our field to support their critical engagement with practice and policy, through the use of evidence based on research and on experience.

In this particular volume Victoria Door draws on her considerable experience as a practitioner in teacher education to examine some of the most challenging ideas that constitute the professional basis of contemporary teaching. 'Criticality' and 'creativity' are words that abound in much education literature, if less commonly in policy texts, but are words which are all too rarely closely examined and analysed in order to inform the learning of beginning teachers. When these two concepts are combined with the third key concept of 'reflexivity' we really do begin to see what it is that can make the work of teachers so exciting and fulfilling – and yet demanding. I think Victoria's book will provide a very strong basis for ensuring that as we enter the new territories of 'school-based' and 'school-led' teacher education, the complexity of teachers' work is not ignored and that the nature of teachers' professional learning is underpinned by sound theory.

Ian Menter, Series Editor
Professor of Teacher Education, University of Oxford
October 2014

About the series editor

Ian Menter is Professor of Teacher Education and Director of Professional Programmes in the Department of Education at the University of Oxford. He previously worked at the Universities of Glasgow, the West of Scotland, London Metropolitan, the West of England and Gloucestershire. Before that he was a primary school teacher in Bristol, England. His most recent publications include *A Literature Review on Teacher Education for the 21st Century* (Scottish Government) and *A Guide to Practitioner Research in Education* (Sage). His work has also been published in many academic journals.

About the author

Victoria Door is based at Keele University, where she works with developing teachers from PGCE to PhD level, including providing continuing professional development (CPD) for whole schools. She is an advocate of keeping educational practice alive and kicking, whether in the classroom or the seminar room, and thinks that one way to do this is to give high priority to practitioners' lived experience and to make reflexivity key.

ACKNOWLEDGEMENTS

I should like to thank all my colleagues involved in Initial Teacher Education at Keele, who have all, directly or indirectly, contributed to this book. I would like to mention particularly Graeme Easdown, who coached my first steps into Master's-level teaching, and Rob Stannard, for the detailed discussions we had prior to and during the writing of this book. I am indebted to Julia Morris at Critical Publishing and to Ian Menter, the series editor, for their comments, feedback and encouragement.

My thanks go to Brian Door, without whose support and inspiration nothing would have been written, to Clare Wilkinson for her insights into teachers and classrooms and to Rose Whyman for showing me it was possible to write a book.

I also wish to thank those PGCE and Master's students who have allowed their words to be used, in particular to Gary and Heather. I hope their contributions will inspire readers to go on developing their own and others' practice.

About this book

Teaching is an extraordinarily difficult job that looks easy.

(Labaree, 2008, pp 298–9)

Who is it for?

This book is intended for all those involved in preparing teachers for the primary and secondary classroom, but I hope that it will be useful both to anyone who is interested in developing their educational practice and to those who would like to share in some of the ideas that have emerged from Keele University's 60 years of experience of teacher development.

Context and approach

We have found that the most successful and enduring approach is one with a coherent underlying ethos (Cruikshank, 1981; Connell and Edwards, 2014). The ideas laid out in this book have been generated at Keele over many years of involvement in teacher preparation, research and professional dialogue within and beyond our current teacher education partnership.

Our ethos is one which emphasises an understanding of what lies behind our pedagogy; that is, the personal, interpersonal, political and cultural context in which we work. We are trying to understand two main things:

1. what it means to be '*more fully human*' (Freire, 1971, p 28) and

2. '*how human beings achieve a meeting of minds, expressed by teachers usually as "how do I reach the children?" or by children as "what's she trying to get at?"*'(Bruner, in Leach and Moon, 2007, p 5).

Teachers and pupils are conceptualised as human beings first, rather than as '*a regime of numbers*' (Ball, 2013, p 103); that is, a source of data used to tell a story of government efficiency and teacher failings (Ozga, 2008). Further, using Bruner's words again, in this ethos pupil and teacher are seen in relation to subject knowledge as '*active, intentional being(s), with knowledge as "man-made" rather than simply there*' (p 19).

As a team of teacher educators, we try to support teachers to base their educational practice on developing a particular '*pedagogical disposition*' (Kruger and Tomasello, in Leach and Moon, 2007, p 6). We have adapted Kruger and Tomasello's idea that humans have a seemingly innate tendency to '*demonstrate correct performance for the benefit of the learner*' (ibid). Our interpretation of the idea is that the fundamental pedagogical disposition can take different forms which connect to our personal and professional beliefs about education.

The aim is not to impose an ethical straightjacket, as that would be contrary to the idea of criticality and creativity. Instead, we try to open up ways of thinking which allow student teachers themselves to develop in relation to primary or secondary pedagogy in a way that takes them far beyond national teacher standards.

Teacher dispositions

The ethos for the dispositions can be distilled into the phrase '*developing practitioners who are reflexive, critical and creative and want their practice to flourish in an on-going way*'. The three basic dispositions are outlined below and developed in the main chapters of the book.

1. A reflexive disposition

Practitioners cultivate awareness of their own pedagogy and a desire to go on developing it. They seek out the means to create and sustain an inclusive learning environment for their pupils, which is engaging, exciting and empowering, so that understanding, knowledge and skills are strengthened and advanced in a way that leads pupils to see that learning really is for life. In creating such a learning environment, teachers practice sensitivity to their own cognitive and emotional needs and to the needs of others. They are able to reflect on their own experiences and values, and respect those of others. At the same time, they want to expand their own and others' cultural and cognitive horizons. They consider what it means to be human.

2. Disposed towards being critical

They take issues of equity and social justice for all seriously. They think in a disciplined way and empower themselves with rigorous subject knowledge. They seek meaning informed by evidence, but do not accept evidence passively, choosing instead to question it actively, seeing it in context. They use all this to exercise good judgements on pedagogy and curriculum which are always taken in the light of '*what it would mean truly to flourish as a human being*' (Higgins, 2010, p 213).

3. Disposed towards being creative

Practitioners use experience, knowledge and sensitivity to think through teaching, learning and curriculum in new ways, allowing scope for informed alternative explanations and conceptions. They practice '*a pedagogy of hope*' (Freire, 2006, p 1) rather than of despondency. They consider it necessary to cultivate their practice and their own development, so that they have a wide and considered perspective to offer to their pupils.

Although pupils are at the centre of what they do, creative practitioners realise they have to nurture their own creativity in order to renew and sustain themselves (Higgins, 2010).

These three dispositions taken together describe what we consider to be the basis of a flourishing educational practice. They could be seen as somewhat rhetorical, but if we take Higgins' argument seriously, that teachers need to cultivate themselves in order to provide the conditions for pupils to flourish, then we can use the 2012 PISA (Programme for International Student Assessment) report to make an economic, as well as a humanist case for the dispositions.

In order to effectively meet the economic, political and social demands for competencies much more is required of students and adults than just cognitive proficiency (Levin, 2012). Consequently, education systems should be evaluated in terms of their capacity to develop all aspects of human potential, ranging from subject-specific achievement to socio-emotional, psychological, ethical and behavioural aspects.

(OECD, 2013, p 21)

Content

In order to avoid writing a book that is largely rhetorical in nature, all the statements regarding the dispositions are based very firmly in the reality of the practice of the Keele-school partnership, consisting of the university and up to 60 secondary schools. All chapters contain practical ideas on how to put this particular professional ethos into practice. But without some link to theory, practical ideas can be simply tips for teachers and lose any connection with a coherent principle. So the ideas put forward do have a theoretical and ethical basis, and have proved fruitful in the reality of our own context of teacher preparation in a British university-school partnership.

Throughout, this book draws on ideas from a range of writers to give a sense of the richness of theory in educational practice. In Chapters 2, 3 and 4, however, the number of thinkers is deliberately restricted to show how specific theories can be used to relate directly to practice. There is some recommended reading at the end of each chapter, which contains publications having particular significance for the topic. The references section at the end of the book contains the authors, dates, titles and publisher of any writing referred to.

CRITICAL **ISSUES**

- *Why call it teacher education?*
- *What is a disposition and why does it matter?*
- *Why do teachers need to go on developing?*
- *Why does development need to start early?*
- *Why is it not selfish to want a flourishing practice?*

Education, not training: what's in a word?

Case study: Joe's lesson

Although it was a cold afternoon, the south-facing classroom was hot and stuffy. Eight Year-10 pupils were spread out amongst the tables for their Spanish lesson; two girls both called Sarah sat with the only two boys of the group, three girls sat at the table next to them and Clara sat at the furthest corner of the furthest table, with her head on her arms and her eyes closed. The student teacher had prepared a model lesson, full of good practice, moving from group activity to a series of competitive games using mini whiteboards, to the core of the lesson, which was 'improving written course-work'. But the pace of the lesson gradually slowed. The two Sarahs had ceased to bother, the boys had worked on a couple of their sentences, nobody seemed quite sure what the three invisible girls at the middle table had done, and Clara was sitting glaring at the two Sarahs. Joe, the student teacher, moved from pupil to pupil, encouraging, asking questions, showing, suggesting ideas, but the pace slowed even more and everybody seemed glad when the bell rang. When the pupils had left, Joe sat despondently on one of the tables. Before the lesson, Joe's school mentor Clare, Joe and myself, as Joe's university tutor, had had a conversation about the relative merits of the term 'teacher training' and 'teacher education'.

Clare: *You have an idea of what teaching is about before you go into it, so it's not a case of being educated like a pupil … You are trained, but your training would differ from school to school … but I suppose the basics of teaching are the same … What's expected is the progress in your class. Making progress, here anyway, is the cornerstone of every lesson. You train someone to do that. How are you going to do that?*

Me: *Well yes! Can you train someone to make a class of various kids from various places and various ages make progress?*

Clare: *Yes. That's what we're here for, isn't it, as teacher trainers?*

Joe: *I think training suggests there's a set way of doing it. If you do it that way, you always get results.*

At the end of the lesson the conversation went like this:

Me: *How do you train someone to deal with a class like that? Is it training or..?*

Clare: *No!*

Joe: *I think training someone is saying there is a set process, do it like that, then do it again and do it again … but I don't think you can do it like that in a school. If you said, right, that's how you have to do it, the next lesson they come in and they'd all be fine and they'd all be getting on. It wouldn't be the same. It's about educating you to make your own decisions based on what you've got, isn't it?*

Teaching is complex and has profound consequences

How we talk about things, the expressions we use, may be revealing of who we are (Chomsky, 2002). Language may also have power to influence how we think and act (Pinker 2007). Because of the potential importance of words, this section looks at the pros and cons of (that is, it critically evaluates) the terms 'teacher training' and 'teacher education'.

Why can it possibly matter whether we train teachers to be teachers or we 'educate' them? Perhaps neither verb is adequate to express the nature of the preparation required to enable adults to take responsibility for the education of children and young people on a year-by-year, day-to-day, minute-by-minute basis. Our experience supports Labaree's claim that '*(t)eaching is an extraordinarily difficult job*' (2008, p 298). Training is not enough because it cannot prepare students for the uncertainties of the profession.

On a daily basis, teachers confront complex decisions that rely on many different kinds of knowledge and judgment and that can involve high-stakes outcomes for students' futures. To make good decisions, teachers must be aware of the many ways in which student learning can unfold in the context of development, learning differences, language and cultural influences, and individual temperaments, interests, and approaches to learning. In addition to foundational knowledge about these areas of learning and performance, teachers need to know how to take the steps necessary to gather additional information that will allow them to make more grounded judgments about what is going on and what strategies may be helpful. Above all, teachers need to keep what is best for the child at the center of their decision making. This sounds like a simple point but it is a complex matter that has profound implications for what happens to and for many children in school.

(Darling-Hammond and Bransford, 2005, pp 1–2)

In that extract there is an emphasis on complex decision-making, and the far-reaching consequences of the judgements teachers make, together with the knowledge needed to make decisions and to have something to teach. I think it gives a sense of why Darling-Hammond and Bransford refer to themselves as 'teacher educators' rather than trainers.

It is thought that the term 'training' gives a sense of teaching as simply working through a *set of mechanical tasks in a routine way* (Ashby, Hobson, Tracey, Malderez, Tomlinson, Roper, Chambers and Healy, 2008, p i) and is associated with a view of teaching where *understanding and intelligent awareness* are not required (Tomlinson, 1995, p 11). So to use the word belittles and underestimates the nature of the profession. There are routines of teaching, like getting pupils in and out of classrooms, taking the register, writing on a board, setting up electronic resources, accessing and entering electronic data. I would not quibble with using the word 'train' in the context of those routines. But this year, for example, my own students reported in an evaluation survey that they 'trained themselves' to do those kinds of activities after having been shown once or twice (Keele, 2014). So we could argue that anyone in the role of 'trainer' is needed only briefly for an initial demonstration, which could easily be done by the classroom teacher or assistant. But if we take Darling-Hammond and Bransford seriously when they claim that teachers *must be aware of the many ways in which student learning can unfold* (2005, p 2) then even carrying out the routines may involve awareness and understanding of how those activities impact upon the range of pupils we have in our care.

Insistence on a particular use of language is in part a political struggle, where teachers maintain that what they do is not simply to 'deliver' the policy of governments or for-profit organisations (Ball, 2013). In our own experience as a teacher education partnership, in our professional conversations with teachers, and from research on teacher perception (Cassell, 2014; James, 2006; James and Pedder, 2006; Marshal and Drummond, 2006) teachers may make political points, but do it in order to stick up for a broad, highly principled view of the nature and purpose of the classroom.

This helps to explain why many educationalists use the term 'education' and refer to those who work in preparing teachers as 'teacher educators'. Although it is certain that the learning of routines, or 'training', is part of the whole, there is much more to it than that. On the whole the evidence points to the inadequacy of 'training' as a conceptual term whereas the term 'education' makes us have to think more deeply what we are doing.

Pedagogic dispositions, practical knowledge and consciousness

I suggest that the main advantage of thinking in terms of pedagogic dispositions is that it makes us want to find out what we think and why we do what we do as practitioners. If we want to have a flourishing practice ourselves and enable others to develop one, we need to be aware of how we actually go about our teaching in real terms, and be able to express it. Much discontent is voiced by our student teachers if they suspect that they are being told one thing and yet see something different in practice. This may be part of the reason that anything that could be classed as 'theory' gets a bad reputation (Holland, Evans and Hawksley, 2011; Waghorn and Stevens, 1996) and that the word 'education' in connection with teacher preparation is distrusted. As Ashby et al (2008) point out:

there is also baggage associated with this term, in that some 'teacher educators' associate the term 'education' more with the learning of declarative knowledge (also known as descriptive or propositional knowledge – 'knowing that') than with the acquisition of procedural knowledge (knowledge exercised in the performance of a task – 'knowing how').

(Ashby et al, 2008, p vi)

I suggest there is a strong connection between propositional and practical knowledge and that the two must go together if we want on-going development. In using these terms, although we are considering routine action in the classroom, we are already in the field of the philosophy of education.

Another way to think about knowing what we are doing in the classroom is by using the terms 'practical' and 'discursive' consciousness. Anthony Giddens (1991), looking at our psychology from the point of view of a sociologist, suggests we have very general awareness of, and trust in, how we do things in everyday life. We could be more aware if we chose but much of the time we have a sense that we can just get on without thinking about it too much. He calls this '*non-conscious*' (p 35) rather than unconscious, as if it were truly unconscious we just wouldn't be able to think about it at all. Practical consciousness has '*tacit or taken-for-granted qualities ... which allow actors to concentrate on the tasks at hand*' (p 36). If we need to monitor what we are doing more closely, we can bring it to 'discursive consciousness'. One way of doing that is by explaining what we are doing and why, to ourselves or to someone else.

Up until the 1980s (Cruikshank 1981) students learning to teach in universities like our own would do courses in the philosophy and sociology of education; this could be called the 'liberal' approach to teacher education. It may be that there was not a close enough focus in those courses upon what their content could possibly have to do with how to teach Year 10 on a Thursday afternoon. Subsequently, the liberal or humanist parts of teacher education courses diminished and they became more competency-focused (Labaree, 2008; Waghorn and Stevens, 1996).

But since the 1980s there has been a lot of research on what it is to learn to teach, on the nature of the demands in the classroom (eg Alexander, 2010; John, 2000; Troman, 1996; Turner-Bissett, 1999) and there is emerging evidence that teachers do need to know 'how' in some areas, and they also need to question that 'how', change it for the better if necessary and be able to justify that change. In response, we seek to integrate philosophy, psychology and sociology in a new way in our teacher education and Master's-level courses, with the aim of raising pedagogical self-awareness. Those three disciplines are put firmly in the service of real-life practice. For example, there are classroom and school routines, ways of using equipment but, as illustrated at the start of the chapter, there are no failsafe, set routines for leading young people towards progress. Moment-by-moment decision-making is a key feature of teaching. These decisions are fundamental to our classroom practice, that is, the way that we have of doing everything that we do in our role as a teacher. Why do we need to know what we are doing? Surely we just need to get on and do it?

Well, not if we are responsible for the education of teachers, as we need to be able to model what we believe and justify that belief to our students. Notice I am suggesting that our actions are based on our beliefs. We can have espoused beliefs (Liang and Dixon, 2011), for example the values we claim to believe in. But it can be argued that an espoused belief is nothing but rhetoric if it is not actually enacted in our practice. If we are not aware of the beliefs that underlie our actions, we can call them implicit beliefs. That mixture of implicit belief, knowledge and understanding we can call our learning theories, and it appears that our learning theories underlie our actions in the classroom (see the discussion in Hargreaves, 1995; Torrance and Pryor, 2001; Twing, Boyle and Charles, 2010).

As we will see from Dewey and Bourdieu in the next chapter, both habit and underlying learning theory intertwine to be very powerful drivers of our classroom practice. Both students and teachers can have ways of doing things in the classroom that just don't seem productive, and the job of the teacher educator is to help them change. Awareness in this context can be thought of as thinking propositionally, or discursively, about classroom practice. It is a way of dredging up implicit beliefs, checking them out to see if they are actually useful, and either getting rid of them, or modifying them. Chapter 2 explores how we can do that, using John Dewey's and Pierre Bourdieu's work on habit, thinking, and the way we position ourselves in the immediate and wider context in which we work.

Reflection

Try to catch yourself making a decision during your everyday practice which involves how you relate to another person. Afterwards, reflect on that decision and any apparent consequences of the action taken. See if you can identify the basis upon which you made that particular choice. Can you put into words what you did, why and what happened?

Pedagogic dispositions and critical understanding

Teachers' work is complex and demanding, and it does seem that an approach which provides only basic classroom competencies will be insufficient to prepare for a practice which goes on developing. Lawes, a language teacher educator, points out that it may not be possible to have a basic competence in the classroom without 'a broader, critical understanding' (2003, p 22) of economic, cultural and political issues. Our experience leads us to agree with Lawes that without such a perspective, classroom practice is impoverished. Teachers need to have a wider awareness of the positioning of the child in society, as well as of their own positions as human beings and educators (their implicit and espoused beliefs, and how those manifest in their own behaviour), together with the intellectual tools for a deep understanding of how policy impacts on curriculum content and methodology, and on themselves as human beings. This position echoes that of influential theorists on the need for intellectual development as part of teacher education (eg Dewey, 1933; Freire, 1971; Giroux, 1988; Hargreaves, 2013). For thinkers such as those referenced above, developing our inherent curiosity about the world is fundamental to pedagogy.

The key word here is 'developing': naïve curiosity may kill a cat, but a critical disposition harnesses our inquisitive nature and sets it to a judicious questioning of both ourselves and the world. An understanding of the kind of questioning found in educational research traditions within higher education offers a framework for our naïve curiosity and a possibility of making our inquisitiveness more informed. It becomes, as Paulo Freire calls it, 'epistemological curiosity' (Freire, 1998 p 35). Currently the European-wide directive on raising the status of school teaching to one equivalent to Master's level (Bologna, 1999) obliges teacher educators in Europe to enable student teachers to engage with academic criticality. Chapter 3 looks at how we can build a very practice-orientated form of academic criticality, which is underpinned by issues of value and ethics, and a general consideration of the big questions, 'what is education for?' and 'why is schooling like it is?'

Pedagogic dispositions and beliefs

The suggestion so far in this chapter has been that teachers need to develop a particular set of pedagogic dispositions, which are an expression of an ethical and practical attitude. They will tend to determine the extent to which a teacher copes in a creative way with the complex nature of teaching, whether their teaching practice flourishes (grows, and goes on growing, in a way that benefits teachers and pupils) and whether that flourishing will be sustained over time. There has also been a hint that helping others to learn involves questioning prior beliefs about how and why things are done in the classroom and in the wider school and educational community.

The importance for teacher educators of understanding the role of belief is highlighted in a major study, published in Britain in 2008, which looked at over a hundred research projects from a range of countries, tracking the experiences of teachers from the start of their preparation to four years in-post. This meta-review of the research literature (Ashby et al, 2008) was commissioned by the government of the time and was looking essentially at the state of teacher preparation in relation to retention. One of the questions asked concerned the influence of teachers' beliefs about their initial preparation and subsequent practice. It emerged that what teachers bring to their preparation, in terms of beliefs about their role, what learning is and how it happens, is hugely significant for how they develop those elements in practice. For example, our prior experience, and knowledge based on that experience, can make us more or less receptive to instruction and guidance in the initial stages of preparation. They will also have an impact on how a developing teacher thinks about issues of control in the classroom and about which models of learning they adopt. Chapter 4 is an exploration of how to question and develop the notion of creativity, suggesting that a fundamental part of that questioning is knowing what we believe about the nature of classroom control. It may seem odd to associate creativity and control, but how we see the role of the teacher in terms of the distribution of power has important implications for creative practice. It is suggested that what we believe can get in the way of being creative and of encouraging others to be so. The issue of belief is explored further in Chapter 5 where we also look at educational enquiry, another essential part of Master's level work.

Starting early

Research on initial teacher education in the United States, England and Finland indicates that a capacity to develop practice in an on-going way needs to be encouraged from the start. If this is the case, and our experience suggests that it is, teacher educators need to encourage practical and propositional knowledge development early in order for it to have any chance of persisting into the teaching career (Scannell, 1999; Darling-Hammond, 1998, 2006; Lawes, 2003; Tryggvason, 2009; Hallet, 2010; Dickson, 2011; BERA-RSA, 2014). That means that there must be space for discussing and practising both from the very early stages of becoming a teacher.

Our suggestion for doing this is to develop the seemingly simple, routine, practical skills within a more complex framework. An example would be learning to write on a board or screen at the front of the classroom while maintaining the attention of the class with an explanation. Such a basic activity requires forming the letters legibly at the same time as speaking, and with that, keeping an awareness of that particular class, who they are, what they are doing and what our attitude towards them is. On our courses, we start by asking student teachers to do at least two of those things at the same time. As soon as possible, they should add the more complex third. This might seem counter-intuitive; surely we should master basic skills one by one before going on to manage three kinds of activity (motor, verbal and awareness)? Well, yes and no. We need to enable student teachers to develop a set of motor skills, but not in isolation from a bigger picture.

We are teaching people to work in a complex environment, to do a lot at one moment, and what we want to avoid is learning one way of doing it which won't then allow for that 'way' to change. Change seems to be more possible if we know from the start what we are doing and why, so we can go back and consider the way we do them. Having said that, I would like to emphasise that we do not want to be verbalising actions in our head while we do them, except under particular conditions, such as demonstrating a skill to students. Our attention when teaching needs to be on what we are doing, in the way Giddens indicates in his concept of practical knowledge. The propositional knowledge is exercised before or after the action if necessary; that is, when we are trying to improve on it. There is emerging evidence that we will have more control over what we do if we are aware of it (Twing et al, 2010), so the aim of our propositional knowledge is to give us control over our classroom practice, and the earlier we start with that sort of reflection-in-action (Schön, 1987) the better.

Reflection

If you think back to how you learned to teach, what did you pick up which you now take for granted? Take one skill or area of understanding that you now feel very secure in and see if you can remember what you had to do in order to learn it at the start.

Is it selfish to want your practice to flourish?

Chris Higgins, writing in the field of the philosophy of education, points out that teaching can be regarded as an altruistic *'helping profession, where caring teachers assist active learners'* (2010, p 190). If teachers do care, and our own experience with our students indicates that they do, we might think that we must channel all our time and energy into helping our pupils. If we do not do that, then we are somehow cheating them, failing to live up to our own ethical standards. Higgins' argument is that if we don't take the time and have the situation where we can cultivate ourselves, we will have little to offer our pupils, and we will suffer from burn-out. The following chapters give ideas for how and why teacher educators need to cultivate themselves and thus be better able to help those for whom they have responsibility. In other words, we need to apply the ideas to ourselves, rather than just telling our students to do them. Then we will be practising what we preach (Hallet, 2010).

IN A **NUTSHELL**

This chapter has demonstrated the importance of the terms we use in teacher education and how they can indicate different ways of thinking about it. It has suggested that if we think about education being humanistic, or people-centred, then an approach where teachers cultivate underlying dispositions seems to prepare them well for the complex and demanding nature of the profession. By finding an underlying ethos for practice, technical skills, or basic classroom competencies, can be learned together with a wider consideration of what is involved in pedagogy. Teachers' beliefs and values play an integral part in learning to carry out even simple routine actions and therefore need to be accessed, and susceptible to challenge and change.

If we want teachers to keep on using insights into themselves and the classroom to move their practice forward, it is necessary to start the process early on. It is possible for teachers to cultivate a sustainable and flourishing practice consciously and it should not be considered selfish to do so.

The core aim of this book is to suggest that one way of cultivating such an on-going practice is to think about the way we are disposed to think and act; that is, to consider our ethical dispositions. The dispositions towards being reflexive, critical and creative were laid out at the start. Of course, labelling these dispositions is simply a way of probing them, of thinking critically about them; that is, of problematising what it is to be an educator. There will be some overlap. For example, approaching the very difficult issues in education in a creative way, with hopefulness, may be informed and tempered by criticality. Criticality includes a willingness to look at our own practice and use the wider views we get from reading to inform and change it. Used in that way, it is a tool for effectiveness. Reflexivity is a disposition of awareness of self and world, realising our own unique attributes and experience and that of others, and must be grounded in caring both for others and ourselves, so that we can cope with being sensitive and accommodating to the needs of others by maintaining our own flourishing practice and life project (Baiasu, 2013; Higgins, 2010).

Having said that, things sometimes have to be divided up for the sake of clarity. The book starts with reflexivity, which deals with the issue of awareness of ourselves as situated in and interacting with the world as we meet it in the classroom. It then moves on to criticality in Chapter 3 and creativity in Chapter 4. Finally, the last chapter draws all the threads together and suggests ways for both teacher educators and developing teachers to research their own practice, using enquiry and the ethical dispositions from the earlier chapters.

REFLECTIONS ON **CRITICAL ISSUES**

- *The word 'education' gives a better sense of the process student teachers need to go through in order to become good practitioners than 'training'.*
- *Dispositions are the underlying attitudes we have towards classroom practice. They are very influential on our pedagogy.*
- *Teaching is such a complex act that we can never know if we have mastered it. Thinking about teaching as an on-going learning process keeps our practice alive.*
- *Student teachers need to start developing the understanding and skills of complex practice from the start, so that a developmental attitude becomes established.*
- *A practice which does not develop becomes stale. A flourishing practice gives the best possibilities to teachers, their pupils and schools.*

Further reading

Freire, P (1998) *Pedagogy of Freedom*. Oxford: Rowman and Littlefield. See Chapter 4, 'Teaching is a Human Act'.

Holland, M, Evans, A and Hawksley, F (2011) International Perspectives on the Theory-Practice Divide in Secondary Initial Teacher Education. Paper delivered at the Annual Meeting of the Association of Teacher Educators in Europe, University of Latvia. [online] Available at: www.shu.ac.uk/_assets/pdf/ceir-ATEE2011-theory-pract-MikeHolland.pdf (accessed 14 April 2014).

CHAPTER 2 | DEVELOPING REFLEXIVE PRACTITIONERS

CRITICAL **ISSUES**

- *What is the difference between a reflexive and a reflective practitioner?*
- *How can Dewey's concept of reflection lead us to reflexivity?*
- *Why do we need to have an understanding of how and when to change our own practice?*
- *How can Bourdieu's concept of 'field' be used to help analyse the very complex situation in which we find ourselves working?*
- *How can Bourdieu's concept of habitus be used to help us see our learned, automatic responses to situations, and does this matter?*

Introduction

This book started with the premise that if beginning teachers are to have a flourishing and sustainable practice, then teacher educators have to provide conditions where they can approach learning to teach as an on-going process of development. The rationale for such an approach is that the capacity to continue developing is necessary in situations where change provides the main element of certainty. The capacity needs to be developed from the start of the preparation for being a teacher, and that puts certain demands on our own professional learning. In this chapter, the meaning of 'reflexivity' is unpacked to show the fundamental importance it has in relation to the on-going development of the critical and creative teacher.

The aim in being reflexive is to be a better educator by understanding ourselves and the setting in which we operate. Reflexive practice, as conceived in the book, means striving to be aware of the impact our actions might be having on others and on the systems in which we work. It also means recognising the external factors which constrain or shape our actions. It demands awareness of our own position on what knowledge is (epistemology), how we define reality (ontology), and of what values we hold on education (axiology or ethics). (These key terms are defined further in the section 'But what is research' in Chapter 5.) It is suggested that the ability to be reflexive is a prerequisite for having that critical dimension discussed in Chapter 3.

The notion of reflexivity is explored using concepts taken from two main thinkers, John Dewey and Pierre Bourdieu. The account given in this chapter is intended to show that although reflection is a major element of being reflexive, it is necessary to go beyond it.

A little background is given on both theorists, and then an indication of how theory might be used to deepen understanding of practice, together with comments from teachers who have tried it.

Reflecting on practice: what's the use?

Getting teachers to reflect has become an integral part of mainstream teacher education and continuing professional development (eg Zeichner and Liston, 2014; Moore, 2007). There is a range of publications on teacher reflection in the further reading section of this chapter, including Dewey's (1933) book for teachers, *How We Think,* referred to below. You are encouraged to read them if you would like to know more about the different perspectives.

In the first chapter I stated that the competency-based model of teacher training was insufficient for the task of developing teachers for the complexity of twenty-first century education, suggesting that perspective and principle are positive dispositions for the flourishing of practice in education. For those dispositions, it is necessary to understand how to use theory in practice. Reflection is a good place to start as it can lead straight into theory, which has to be related to practice as without it there is nothing to reflect on.

Dewey's theories on reflection are discussed here because it is possible to trace many of the ideas in the literature on reflection in education back to him (see eg the first chapter of Zeichner and Liston, 1996). In the spirit of critical questioning, but with '*a generous heart*' (Freire, 1998, p 39), we should of course evaluate all theoretical approaches to see if they are applicable to our own situations. In a reflexive approach, any theory we intend to use as a tool for action in the world must be evaluated before and during use. Both the main theorists in this chapter, Dewey and Bourdieu, expected critique and were aware that they were asking readers to develop tools of questioning which they could use both on their settings and on themselves (see Dewey's introduction to the second edition of *How We Think* (1933) and Bourdieu's *Sketch for a Self-Analysis* (2004/8).

The basics in supporting student teachers in reflection using Dewey's theory

Dewey wrote *How We Think* specifically for teachers (1910, revised 1933). He based his writing initially on his own and his wife's experience of setting up and directing the Chicago University Laboratory School, combined with his own developing views on the philosophy of education and its relation to human nature and democracy. The later version of the book was produced after he had reformulated his thinking as a result of stringent critique from teachers who had read it, together with the changes in both education and his own thinking since the start of the twentieth century. It may seem odd to look at theory developed in the nineteenth century for use in the twenty-first, but we are examining the principles of his work to see if they still hold true, and have some root in the human condition as it is now seen today.

Dewey advocated *'engaged liberalism'* (Aronowitz, 1993, p 10), being both a philosopher and a social activist. For example, he was instrumental in founding and supporting organisations promoting racial equality and educational workers' rights and chaired the commission on Trotsky's murder (Martin, 2002). Dewey's stated concern in the book is to get teachers to think more clearly about what is meant by 'thinking', and specifically, to indicate the value of reflective thinking for educators.

Reflection starts with *'a state of doubt, hesitation, perplexity'* (Dewey, 1933, p 12) which leads to enquiry with a purpose. The idea of this two-stage process is much developed in the literature (eg Schön, 1983, 1987; Moon, 2004). Enquiry does not have to be a big thing; essentially, says Dewey, it can start with something very small, such as looking up at the sky to see why the temperature has dropped. He gives another example of coming to a junction in a road and wondering which way to turn. The choice depends on where we want to go. If we don't actually care where we end up, or are confident that we know which road to take, no reflection is needed.

Relating this idea straight to practice, in our own institution we can see its influence on the way student teachers are asked to reflect after a lesson.

1. *'How do you think that went?'* is sufficient stimulus to start the process of looking up at the sky.

2. *'What would you have changed and why?'* is a more searching stimulus.

3. *'What was the most challenging part of the lesson for pupils?'* or

4. *'What messages did the lesson convey about your subject?* are intended to cause a student 'some perplexity'.

(adapted from Dewey, 1933, p 15)

These probes have been designed to encourage a student teacher to review what happened, both in the classroom and before that, in the planning of a lesson. They provide a framework of enquiry into what is in fact a very complex set of thoughts, actions and consequences. The point of lesson evaluation, or review, is to enable development. Hopefully it will be possible for students using reflective thinking both to act differently and to see more the next time, providing they do some *'careful and extensive study upon purposeful widening of the area of observation'* (Dewey, 1933, p 8). The aim is to change something, which may be a very specific thing, like remembering to take the register, monitoring the voice, or trying a different sequence of steps in the explanation of a concept, and then to review what happened.

It may be surprising to think of 'belief' in terms of how teachers take the register, but Dewey is quite clear that our actions are physical manifestations of our beliefs (and we see the same idea in Bourdieu, later in the chapter). So the tone of voice used in the classroom stems from the way the teacher thinks about the act of talking to her learners. To change our voice means to change that belief. Dewey's reflection commits us to challenging our beliefs. The commitment rests on that *'careful and extensive study upon purposeful widening of the area of observation'* (ibid), which involves us in challenging both how we think about reality (our ontology) and how we think about what we know (our epistemology).

This reasoning process leads to distrust of the beliefs we hold but perhaps never question, and to challenging them on the basis of evidence. Negative feedback from an observer on a physical manifestation, such as the tone of voice, might cause us sufficient 'perplexity' to dare to examine a belief actively. That feedback, combined with a willingness to listen to our voice the next time we teach, makes our reflection evidence-based. Many of our beliefs have been picked up without our knowing:

(f)rom obscure sources and by unnoticed channels they insinuate themselves into the mind and become unconsciously part of our mental furniture ... such thoughts are prejudices; that is prejudgements not conclusions reached as a result of personal mental activity, such as observing, collecting and examining evidence.

(Dewey, 1933, p 7)

It is because our actions are based on our beliefs, which we may be more or less attached to, that it is not simple to change practice. We need to see something and be prepared to think differently. Donald Schön, who did his PhD on Dewey's theory of enquiry (see Schön, 1992) and wrote two very widely used books on reflection (see Schön, 1983, 1987), coined the phrase '*reflection-in-action*' for being able to catch yourself in the moment. It is likely he developed this concept from Dewey's '*thinking-in-activity*' (Alexander, 1985, p 42), but he left out that crucial component of the influence of belief. It is in this juncture of awareness of belief, thought and action that I think Dewey leads us from simple reflection to reflexivity. Awareness of how we are acting in the moment and being prepared to change are central if we want to keep our classroom practice developing, but it takes time, and from our partnership experience, it also requires a great openness to learning and humility regarding one's own expertise, whether we are starting out as teachers, or working as teacher educators.

Increasing the scope of reflection

Another important strand of Dewey's theory of reflection is that it is purposeful, rather than random or simply associative; it is consecutive and '*con-sequential*' (Dewey, 1933, p 4) so that '*(e)ach phase is a step from something to something ... There are in any reflective thought definite units that are linked together so that there is a sustained movement to a common end*' (Dewey, 1933, pp 4–5). This is not a linear way of thinking; it is about being able to think through many possible alternatives to a problem. But we also have to be critical of the ideas which occur to us, requiring '*(a)ctive, persistent and careful consideration of any belief or supposed form of knowledge in the light of the grounds that support it and the further conclusions to which it tends*' (Dewey, 1933, p 9). Again, this is not necessarily a quick process. We have to be '*willing to endure suspense and undergo the trouble of searching ... to sustain and protract that state of doubt which is the stimulus to thorough inquiry*' (p 16).

In other words, there's no value in quickly marshalling a lot of ideas which support what we actually want to happen (as opposed to what might be the 'best' answer, if in fact there is one). We have to be prepared to take as much of the available information into account as we can in coming to any final judgement on what to do. Although by this process we are trying to find what Dewey sees as a rational solution (in terms of best fit to the issue), developing the different skills of insight and discernment, which are part of learning the essential 'good' judgement, defined as that which leads to the 'best' solution.

Clearly, in searching for a solution, we need to know what problem it is that needs solving. Here we encounter what Dewey called 'ends'. But who decides the 'end' and who the means of getting there? Here we come to the junction of reflexivity and criticality. As individual educators, we have the freedom to decide our own personal code of conduct, which consists of our beliefs about how we should behave, and thus influences which ends we choose (our ethics or axiology). For example, it would be reasonable to suggest that an appropriate personal code for a teacher is one which prevents them from imposing anything upon a learner by threats, by fear, or to take any action which is not clearly in the best interest of the learner's well-being. Our experience of beginning teachers leads us to believe that the vast majority of those who go into the profession really do want the best for their pupils, in theory, even if that does not always hold up in practice. Being reflexive means trying to see how a personal code of wanting good for others can translate into practice in the classroom. It is this 'end' we are looking for, then, in learning to teach. We need to see how we, or external factors, might get in the way of that goal, and take decisions about how we might change ourselves, or those factors.

Consecutive thinking may sound dull and something we do anyway, but it immediately raises the issues of values, personal and professional ethics and indeed the ethics of policy, all of which are looked at again in Chapter 3. But there is also something else: Dewey's insistence on reflection as something we need to persist with, whether it is a short-term or a long-term end. How often do we, as educational practitioners, take the long view of a pupil starting schooling, in terms of their whole school career, going on to the post-16 phase? If we do, do we think of it in terms of what our end, or goal, is for that pupil? Asking that question should immediately reveal our ethical standpoint. What do we think education is for? What do we think our role as a teacher is in that view? What are our 'ends' for our learners? On what basis do we make decisions on the kind of schooling experience any particular child should have? Do we behave differently when we deal with learners we like less than others? If we do, how does that fit with our ethical principles as an educator? Are we able, and willing, to think through the consequences of our actions in the classroom in terms of the longer-term well-being of pupils? These are reflexive questions we should raise with ourselves, even if we don't find definitive answers. We raise all of these questions with our student teachers and give them a forum for discussing them.

It is common practice on teacher education courses to start students thinking through short activities such as planning a starter for a lesson. Students then graduate to planning half a lesson, then a whole lesson, a sequence of lessons, a term's work and then a scheme of work for a year. In working with a simple gradualist approach, we could run the risk of putting limits on consecutive thought, by not encouraging the long view. In order to avoid that, we ask students at the very start of the course to reflect forward on the kind of teacher they would like to become.

Reflection

Think of the elements of your practice you would most like to be known for. Choose one of these and see if you can actually see yourself practising it during your everyday work. Consider how you would teach that particular element to someone else.

Moving towards reflexivity using Dewey's theory

Viewed in one way, Dewey is proposing a procedure, a chain of steps in thinking and review which can lead to change in a move towards a particular goal. But to suppose that it stops there, or that there is a simple mechanical answer to classroom practice, or to educating classroom practitioners, is to mistake its nature. Schön writes about the growing realisation in the 1970s that what he calls *'technical rationality'* (Schön, 1983, Chapter 2) was inadequate for situations which arise in a profession such as teaching. Why? Because of:

[t]he changing character of the situations of practice – the complexity, uncertainty, instability, uniqueness and value conflicts ... perceived as central to the world of professional practice.

(Schön, 1983/2011, p 14)

I could elaborate that 'situations' in education involve both policy (politics) and people, including politicians, managers, teachers, learners and parents, all of whom may see different purposes generally in education and specifically in schooling. A simple view of reflection as something which throws the responsibility for all ills in the classroom onto the teacher needs to be questioned in such a context.

One of the criticisms levelled against the use of 'reflection' for teachers is that it is a technique of self-surveillance as described by Foucault in his book *Discipline and Punish*, first published in 1975, and thus can be used not for self-control and personal development, but for domination by another person or group. However, I see surveillance techniques, whether done by others or by the self on behalf of others (Ball, 2013), as inimical to the individual's flourishing practice.

Another criticism we should consider is that reflection in initial teacher education is used as a substitute for theory, so that reflecting on practice equates to theorising about it (McIntyre, 1995; Zeichner and Liston, 2014; Lawes, 2003). In one sense, that is true and it is what we want; to take our practice, think deeply and widely about it and generalise some principles from it. The danger here is that reflecting can be a subjective, self-referential process (Lawes, 2003). We suggest that it requires a wider knowledge of other people's thoughts on experience, including research, which have been held up to public scrutiny and found to be of value. Peer review, which all the published literature quoted in this book has been subject to, supplies such a process. The subjectivity of individual reflection alone is not enough. Reflexivity is the recognition by individuals that the very cognitive tools with which they reflect may have been constituted by a professional discipline (ie here, education in the widest sense) and cannot themselves be easily separated from what Bourdieu calls 'state thinking' (Bourdieu, 2004, p 91), and that those tools may be subject to critical examination. Teachers who simply learn to reflect on their own actions may fall between two equally undesirable stools: self-referential individualism, an 'individualistic response to problems' (Lawes, 2003, p 25), which can include being too self-critical (Grenfell, 1998), and ignorance of the external political and cultural factors which they have internalised, and which shape in a very real way the environment in which they work.

In summary, reflection is an essential element of reflexivity, but we have to move beyond a simple conception of reflection to one which is liberating for the individual, rather than controlling – one which occurs through increasing capacity of awareness, together with the exercise of intelligent responsibility for creative ends (Freire, 1972). Dewey thought that the way teachers think is hugely important for the flourishing of their pupils, but also for society, and thus for all of us (Dewey, 1938). He goes as far as suggesting that:

Genuine freedom is intellectual; it rests in the trained power of thought, in ability to 'turn things over', to look at matters deliberately, to judge whether the amount and kind of evidence requisite for such decision is at hand, and if not, to tell where and how to seek such evidence.

(1933, p 90)

I want to add something to that, which I think you can find in reading Dewey, but which is not often brought out, which is that we need to become aware of our own particular viewpoint, our bias, you could say, and how that influences our choice of evidence. Can we escape from our own bias? Do we even want to? These are questions which Bourdieu's concepts of 'field' and 'habitus' can help us answer.

Supporting student teachers towards reflexivity using Bourdieu's theory

Interpretations of Bourdieu's thinking are much used in educational research at Master's and doctoral level. His is a conceptual approach, but a very particular one, which is not 'theoretical' as he was firmly opposed to theoreticism (Bourdieu and Wacquant, 1992, p 26) His conceptualisation is, it is claimed, pragmatic; he treats concepts as tool kits 'designed to help him solve problems' (p 31). This may be why some of Bourdieu's thinking is useful for developing educational practitioners in a way that combines theory and on-the-ground practice. Bourdieu was a sociologist, with a very deep grounding in philosophy. As with reading any writer of theory, we need to bear his background in mind and realise that we are trying to apply it to a particular area of human culture, that of educational practice.

Developing reflexivity using 'field'

What follows is a simple and personal version of reflexivity developed for use with pre- and in-service teachers. Bourdieu's own descriptions are of course much more complex and we recommend that you read his work (see further reading) if you would like to dig deeper.

For Bourdieu, reflexivity involves the individual's realisation of our formation by social institutions: not only static ones, like the school we attended, but also more abstract ones, like 'education', which we pick up from the cultural environment in which we are brought up. Our own teachers, parents and social contacts and peers were all formed in their turn, and brought their theories about educational practice into contact with us during our formative years. Reflexivity demands that we (and our students) analyse the local and national institutions in which we work. However, any institution we try to analyse cannot be studied in isolation. It is 'nothing outside its relations to the whole' (Bourdieu and Wacquant, 1998, p 232).

Bourdieu suggests that such environments of organised human culture can be thought of in terms of a 'field', for example the scientific field, the economic field, or the field of education. Each field is 'a space of play and competition' (Bourdieu and Wacquant, 2008, p 76). There are rules for each field but, nevertheless, room for change. It is possible to view the rules as structures, which actually exist (they are objective) but are maintained by decisions taken by those with the power, with the consent (conscious or unconscious) of others in the field. We can think of fields of different sizes, so that all of a country's educational system could be the main field with subfields of the different, more specialised areas, like secondary, private or state-maintained education, nested within it. In any field or subfield at any moment in time, there are structures which are created and maintained by some kind of agreement from the players. The structures are maintained relative to the power of the groups and individuals within the field. What Bourdieu is trying to describe is that each area of human activity has its own particular characteristics, but those characteristics are not fixed. Rather, they are in a state of potential flux brought about by the vying for power among those who are considered members of that field. The fields are not watertight; they are in dynamic relation with elements of other fields, for example the educational field in England is not separate from the national economic field, nor from the global one. The more autonomous a field, the more freedom it has to create its own rules and structures. It is worth considering how autonomous our own particular area of education might be, and the potential a teacher at any particular stage of their career has in maintaining or changing structures. Autonomy in a field is something desired by the members of that field, but challenged by others, particularly in what Bourdieu called 'the field of power' (Bourdieu, 1993, p 38), by which he meant the wilder and greater space in which those with most power play. Education globally is a space which fights for its autonomy, but is continually dominated by government and, increasingly, business (Ball, 2012; Howlett, 2013). Such a state of affairs is relevant to the reflexive practitioner as they try to understand what parts of their own practice are autonomous.

We can use the concept of having a personal field as a tool to get teachers thinking about the complexity of what they might see as simply 'classroom practice', at the same time as trying to understand the wider field in which they are working, that of education. To that end, we ask teachers at different stages of their careers to map out their practice on paper. They start with themselves as teacher in the centre and move out, noting all the structures (people, rules, situations) with which they directly or not-so-directly come into contact. The wider fields are then apparent as we bump into them in our map-making. In the words of one of our Master's students, an ICT ((information and communication technology) teacher of six years' experience at the time of interview, the mapping exercise '*starts you thinking about where you are coming from and the misconceptions that you bring into the realms of the classroom*' (Caroline, 2013).

We need to emphasise again, as does Bourdieu, that this concept is just a tool, in this case to be used to try and see something about classroom practice more clearly and to be able to act in some way that we, as individual practitioners, think improves it.

Reflection

Take a large piece of paper, or use a software mapping application. Put your own practice at the centre and then map on all the things you have to do, all the rules, people and situations that you have to deal with. Add to it from time to time when you think of something further or get asked to do something more.

Developing reflexivity using 'habitus'

Bourdieu wonders at the relative stability of fields; although they do change over time, there seems to be a tendency for things to stay the same. He suggests that one element of this seems to be a characteristic of reflexivity in terms of social structures, that is, the potentially circular nature of how we set things up, which in turn determines how they will be set up in the future: '*(T)he organization of society gives rise to ideas which in turn shape the organization of society*' (Grenfell, 1998, p 10). But the other element essential to the maintenance of a field is the nature of the agents within it. We, as agents, all have our own freedom of thought and action, but largely the way we both think and act is defined by the social environment in which we grew up. This is not simply 'conditioning', whereby we respond to the world in a way typical for our social background, but a deeply ingrained part of who we are. Bourdieu named this 'habitus'.

Case Study: Gary's experience of habitus

Bourdieu was at pains to explain that his concept of habitus points to something very real; it is not meant simply to designate something mental or our actions in the world. Habitus is the way we, as individuals, look at the world, the way the world seems to us, together with our voice, posture, ways of moving, gestures, emotional and physiological responses. One of our MA students, a maths teacher and assistant head, was particularly struck by the connection of thought and bodily response. He reported:

I'm beginning to see things from other perspectives for example in meetings which can become quite heated. I felt myself wanting to argue my case of why all the things that everyone else said were wrong ... and I felt myself becoming warm and heated.

(Gary, 2011)

Gary used reflexivity to escape his habitus. He was able to have insight in the moment and then to think in a different way:

And then I reflected that no, it's a collegial debate and in this instance you have been overruled and then I felt for a little while that I had lost face. But then I thought, you haven't; you've seen other people bring things up and not get them through and you haven't felt any differently towards them ... I feel more empowered in my relationships with colleagues and students, and with failure as well, in being able to rationalise it and not take it personally by being reflexive. I feel empowered when I talk to colleagues ... they are not reflexive and they have no idea how to be reflexive and they are sort of blundering from one point to another.

(Gary, 2011)

Gary saw that our perceptions are 'sedimented' within us; they are corporeal and are *'lodged inside the body'* (Bourdieu and Wacquant, 1998, p 22) waiting to be reactivated. Bourdieu describes how our body has been socialised by the social and cultural fields of its past. Because those fields were all spaces where either people or systems were vying to dominate each other, our current mental and corporeal habits render us complicit in whatever power games were going on around us in our growing up. *'You do things automatically, your muscle memory and you respond to situations automatically'* (Gary, 2011).

Being unaware of such automatic response is particularly relevant because of the impact it can have on us and on our students. Gary's example below shows how we may want to change our habitual reactions to situations as we develop our practice in terms of understanding ourselves and our learners.

When a student does something which you don't feel is appropriate in front of you, it is not necessarily a direct challenge to your authority. And in fact sometimes they think they are interacting with you in a friendly way and you take it wrongly because you don't understand where they are coming from and then tell them off when they have tried in their own way to be friendly towards you. Sometimes their over-friendliness comes out as a bad choice of language and it's not that they are being insulting or abusive but just when they excited or get carried away they choose what I consider to be a poor use of language but it's the best that they've got. But after doing the assignment I realised that I know that student. They are not abusive or offensive, so why have they just chosen that language? It was the only thing they could get in a rush to fit that situation. Before, I would have shouted at them and they would have gone away and never tried it again.

(Gary, 2011)

If we realise that our habitus is causing us problems as a teacher, and want to change something about it, it takes a bit of doing: *'you have to take a long hard look to see the things that you as a person put to the back of your own mind'*, reported Caroline. Gary describes what sounds like a slightly split way of changing habitus in the moment when he says there is:

the person in the moment and the other person who is looking at that person in the moment and trying to say 'are you aware that there are other things impacting on you now over which you don't have much control, but which put you into this situation? And if you realised that, maybe you'd handle the situation a bit better, a bit more intellectually'.

But when questioned over the nature of the split he adds:

When you build up a store of reflexive arguments and principles they are like a tool kit to use whilst you are in the moment which you can draw on, so maybe it's not two separate personalities it's just a box of things you go into and use at that time, which you build up intellectually as you go along … you ask 'Whilst my reactive personality is doing this, is there anything in here which will help me out?'

(Gary, 2011)

It seems that Gary is practising Dewey's genuine freedom here, in using his intellect and having trained his power of thought (Dewey, 1933).

Changing field and habitus enlarges our 'space of possibles'

Habitus has stability, because it is the only way we know how to do things, to be, and we may be unaware of much of it. We have a perception of what it is possible to do in any particular area, within the power games or 'position takings' that go on in any field. Bourdieu calls this our *'space of possibles'* (Bourdieu, 2004, pp 29, 100). This space has some objective reality, it is not just in our habitus as it is the set of possibilities we have due to our background. It is what society will permit us. Bourdieu claims that our 'space of possibles' is greater according to the privilege of our background. Such a claim is interesting for the educational practitioner in considering the purpose of education. The point for the reflexive practitioner is that we need to understand the limits that we put on things, the limits that society might put on us, and where we stand on both of those (our axiological or ethical position). For teachers exploring their own fields of practice, subject area and habitus in order to develop, there is no quick answer – *'we are in "chains", which have to be broken by degree'* (Caroline, 2013) – but it is of tremendous importance.

My field has changed from one that was narrow, restricted not by a picket fence but chains … Although restrictions are still in place the view is wider and the field stretches as far as the eye can see … The original field was formed against the 'education' that I received whilst in secondary school and the middle class system that I was brought up in. The institution was narrow, knowledge was imparted by those who knew better, and they appeared unable to focus on the possibilities that young minds could be opened and not accept the established norms.

(Caroline, 2013)

Habitus and field are both open to change or, put another way, not closed to it. Habitus is a 'set of dispositions', some we may want to keep, some to change and some to develop afresh.

In terms of reflexivity for beginning teachers, our own experience has shown that by the end of a year's preparation, they are beginning to be able to pause in mid-flow in the classroom and change direction (Smith, 2010). They are aware of themselves as shaped by their particular background and of pupils being in the process of being shaped by theirs, that is the role of education in social and cultural reproduction. They have also seen that the classroom is a microcosm set in a particular institution, in turn set in a particular neighbourhood and national and even international contexts. In other words, they have a surface view of reflexivity. Deeper realisations about the nature of reflexivity need more time and experience to become embedded. In the role as teacher educator, however, it is useful to have a wider and more profound view of what we want for our students, and doing some work on reflexivity is a very rewarding professional development opportunity, so it is the deep view that has been outlined above.

IN A **NUTSHELL**

The chapter started with the statement that in order to help student teachers develop the kind of practice which will be critical and creative in a sustainable way, we need to support them in knowing what their own practice consists of and the factors which shape it, of having an awareness of the impact their practice has on others, and in understanding how and when to change practice. I have suggested that such knowledge, awareness and understanding can be called 'reflexivity' and that to encourage it in others, we need to have developed it ourselves. I have tried to show how theory can be used to impact directly on practice; Dewey positions us as being able to change, and from his work we have drawn out the importance of an increased awareness to the detail of our thought and its very direct influence on action. Bourdieu's explanatory device of habitus provides another view on the same idea, with the physical 'sedimentation' of our cultural background keeping us as we are, within the wider fields in which we live and work. We can use both Dewey's and Bourdieu's theories on our socialisation by institutions as theoretical frameworks for deepening our own awareness of the web of influences in which we both embed ourselves and find ourselves embedded by chance of birth. The point is to develop greater perspective on our own practice and our role in developing that of others for a real possibility of changing practice.

REFLECTIONS ON **CRITICAL ISSUES**

• *Reflective practitioners will think about their own actions and consider whether, and how, to improve them. Reflexive practitioners will consider their own actions in the context of their setting, in the classroom, school and more widely. They will try to see how the wider context influences their thinking and actions, and how their thinking and actions influence their context.*

- *John Dewey conceived of reflection in terms of individual enquiry about self and world, with those two elements always interacting. He also advocated increasing awareness of how we think and act so that we can change educational practice.*
- *If practice is to stay fresh, it must change. Change has to be done on an intelligent and constructive basis, taking into account both self and context (world). Practitioners need to look to their own thinking and acting in order to judge what, when and how to change.*
- *Bourdieu's concept of 'field' can be used to help analyse the very complex situation in which practitioners work as it provides a way of seeing self and context in a joined up way.*
- *Bourdieu's concept of habitus can be used to help practitioners see that they have learned cultural and seemingly automatic responses to situations. An appreciation of this allows the individual to respond differently.*

Further reading

Dewey, J (1933) *How We Think*. Boston: Heath.

Moore, A (2007) Beyond Reflection, in Hammersley, M (ed) *Educational Research and Evidence-Based Practice*. Los Angeles: Sage.

Zeichner, K and Liston, D (2014) *Reflective Teaching and the Social Conditions of Schooling*. New York: Routledge.

CRITICAL **ISSUES**

- *What is criticality?*
- *Why is criticality important?*
- *What do others say about criticality?*
- *How do we practise and help others practise criticality?*

Introduction

In Chapter 2, I suggested reflexivity is a prerequisite to criticality. If we are working at reflecting on our particular field of practice in the way described, we are already practising criticality. I put reflexivity first as, in our experience, if we 'do' criticality without looking at the way we actually go about things, it can become an intellectual game, which is really connected to the very practical in-the-moment world of schooling. Like reflexivity, criticality is about asking questions; in fact it is about cultivating curiosity and, carried out in the right way, it leads to creativity.

But it is a big field and in this chapter only some of it can be explored. Hopefully, the exploration will serve as a taste which will make you want to go on exploring, and there are some ideas for further reading at the end. Because this book is for anyone involved in teacher education, criticality is considered in two main arenas of teacher development: academic scholarship and the classroom. Firstly there is a focus on reading and writing critically as called for in the academic context. Then these skills are extended into critical listening and critical practice. The whole is set in a theoretical framework of a theory of educational ethics, and finishes with a set of tools for criticality.

Our PGCE and Master's students have shown us that learning to read, write and listen critically keeps our educational practice developing but, like reflexivity, the process is continuous and best started early. They sometimes make the argument that you cannot be critical until you are an expert. There is some truth in that, but on the other hand, perhaps it is never too soon for adult learners to examine what they think they know, and for them to remember that there are very likely to be alternatives to their thinking. One of our PGCE students half-way through her course described criticality as:

not taking things for granted, looking at alternatives to perhaps what might be our first response ... I think being critical also means to be able to step out of the habitual approach to what you are doing.

(Heather, 2013)

I suggest that teacher educators want to be able to model criticality for students, but I emphasise that we are talking about critiquing the educational field and our field of practice; using criticality is not recommended in the context of family, friends or entertainment.

The main theorist for this chapter is Paulo Freire, but Louise Poulson and Mike Wallace's work on critical reading and writing and John Searle's philosophy of mind are also called on.

Using Freire's theories of critical awareness to support student teachers

Criticality means: 'Questioning, but also thinking about the reason behind our questions'.

(PGCE student, 2013)

Paulo Freire was a Brazilian teacher and educational philosopher, who can be said to be the inspiration for what has come to be called '*critical pedagogy*' (Howlett, 2013, p 247). Freire was particularly concerned that education should lead to a better world in terms of a just society and the flourishing of the individuals who make up society. He perceived that there is a cycle of domination between and within social groups, which does not promote such flourishing, and that education is a major force in perpetuating cycles of domination. Freire's conception of human beings is that although we are capable of great cruelty and selfishness, we also have the opposite potential for kindness and altruism. The 'better' world is one where we choose kindness and selflessness, but we have to be aware of our potential as humans and choose that route purposefully, sometimes on a daily basis. That awareness he called '*conscientisation*' (Freire, 1971, pp 19–20; Freire, 1998, p 55). Making a conscious choice of the better path of our nature is no bad thing, says Freire; it shows we have some freedom to act rather than being constrained by domination or by fate. We are able to be reflexive, seeing ourselves as part of a bigger picture, but for all that we are an important part of that picture as the way we act in the world really does contribute to how things are: '*My role in the world is not simply that of someone who registers what occurs but of someone who has input into what happens*' (Freire, 1998, p 73). For Freire, all teaching is an ethical act, as we have to choose how we relate to our students, as one who dominates others or as one among equals. That choice as a guiding principle and on a moment-by-moment basis is what he sees as our true humanity. That process of choosing is a move towards 'humanisation', in opposition to 'dehumanisation'. Becoming fully human is the ultimate goal of education for Freire.

The ethical teacher does not in any way neglect subject knowledge or intellectual rigour; we should '*deepen our awareness of the world, of facts, of events*' (Freire, 1998, p 55). We must work to become expert in *what* we teach, and be constantly working to be expert in *how* we teach. The point of most teaching is to enable students to have as much access to the world as possible, and that is done by enabling them to become knowledgeable and to know how to know, not by promoting partial knowledge or ignorance (Bruner, 1969). But teachers should be sensitive to the kinds of knowledge that exist; our students' own current knowledge should be valued and built on. Freire's concept of how we do *not* learn has become increasingly well known, as the 'banking' concept, where the teacher transfers knowledge into the heads of students by some kind of act of authority. In rejecting this approach, Freire is very much a constructivist; as learners, we have actively to construct what we know from the information we find or are exposed to; it cannot be poured into our heads, like liquid knowledge (see Chapter 2 of Freire, 1971).

Freire's educational philosophy is firmly based in his belief that we are curious by nature, and what we do, if not prevented, is to ask questions and to find things out. In Freire's view, we can, and should, allow ourselves to go on being curious all our lives. As we grow up, we can temper this curiosity with intellectual discipline, or '*methodological rigour*' (1998, p 35); thus our natural desire to find things out can be transformed into '*epistemological curiosity*' (1998, p 35). In this way, we can hardly help but research as we teach. As we reflect on our teaching we find out what we can change: '*I research because I notice things, take cognizance of them. In so doing, I intervene.*' (Freire, 1998, p 35). The intervention is where we put changes into practice. In this virtuous cycle, we have the power to transform things around us in a benevolent way, thus humanising the world.

Freire's critical pedagogy is the basis of our definition of criticality for teacher educators, as it combines an ethical approach (for the common and individual good) which supplies a 'good' reason for pursuing ever-expanding knowledge and understanding of our field, in whatever subject background we come from, and for asking questions about our own practice and the curriculum and educational policy more widely. In the previous chapter, I looked at questioning our own practice, so I focus here mainly on how knowledge can be questioned, particularly of how that act is conceptualised in higher education. I think that it is possible to see Freire's ideas in the expected standards for postgraduate teacher education and in national curriculum documents, so that nothing said below is revolutionary; it is more about putting rhetoric on democracy, social justice and active learning into practice, however much we may do it imperfectly.

(C)onscientization is a requirement of our human condition. It is one of the roads we have to follow if we are to deepen our awareness of the world, of facts, of events, of the demands of human consciousness to develop our capacity for epistemological curiosity … it is natural to 'unfinished' humanity that is aware of its unfinishedness.

(Freire, 1998, p 55)

Some background on criticality in higher education

There is a European agenda for standardising teacher education at Master's level (Bologna, 1999), matched by the United States (Darling-Hammond, 2005; Grant and Agosto, 2008), Canada (Foley, 2012) and Australia (Aspland, 2006). A similar agenda is emerging in India (IITE, 2014) and China (Guo, 2012). As a consequence, teacher educators globally may have an obligation to enable their students to engage with academic criticality, as well with on-the-ground classroom practice.

Over the past 20 or so years, the idea of exposing teachers-in-training to academic critical practice separately from classroom practice has become discredited in the United Kingdom and the United States (Darling-Hammond, 2006; McIntyre, 2009; Johnston, Ford, Myles, and Mitchell, 2011; Menter, 2013). The challenge for the teacher educator is to be able to use the tools in an academic and practice context and to help others to do so. We can no longer rely on an academic to 'deliver' the theory relating to educational practice; all those involved in teacher education must become critical practice experts, using the term 'critical' to embrace both knowing and being able to use the rules of academic reading and writing in a way that draws on and feeds into classroom practice.

Poulson and Wallace (2004) give a helpful explanation of the global status of criticality in higher education. They report the growing acceptance of criticality as standard in many areas of the world, in a move from an authoritarian, not-to-be challenged model of expert to learner to one where the learner is *obliged* to question the work of the expert. Such an approach spans both humanities and sciences, leading into the global academic checking device of peer review. Any work published in an academic journal is subject to rigorous review by at least two other workers in the field. This does not make the work true, or right, but it does make a statement about the way the author has come to their ideas and their 'reasonableness' within that particular field. It moves work forward from perhaps being the subjective opinion of one person; there has been a process of objectivising the work and giving some assurance that due process has been gone through in the writing of it. Note that it is less the content itself which is under scrutiny, but the evidence and coherence. This allows new ideas to emerge, as long as they are expressed and 'supported' in particular ways.

Reading and writing critically

Poulson and Wallace (2004) suggest that in order to write critically it is necessary to first read critically. I think they are right and want to go further and present critical reading and writing as being directly relevant to the on-going development of practitioner expertise. One obvious direct link is that of keeping up with ideas in teaching and learning. As Tony Eaude puts it:

No one would consult a doctor who did not keep up with medical research, or go to a lawyer who ignored recent judgements. And it would cause an outcry if the government prescribed how a doctor conducted an operation. Yet, such an approach seems acceptable in teaching.

(Eaude, 2012, p 3)

I agree with Johnston, Ford, Myles and Mitchell (2011) that academic writing involves entering into discussions about the ideas of a particular professional area, in this case that of schooling and classroom practice. The discussions are run publicly, that is, in published work, according to rules of the field. The learning of the rules and participation in the discussions can be viewed as '*a key means of practising and expressing criticality*' (p 154).

Reading widely is a way of knowing what has been considered good practice, what is becoming so, and on what basis it is considered 'good'. It is a means to keep subject knowledge current and to refresh areas of it that may have been neglected. In this sense it is very much about reading for information. For example, one year, when teaching critical reading, we asked our students what their first aim in reading is. Ninety per cent said it was to find something out. So we build on that motivation of curiosity, even if it is simply to find out how to pass an assignment.

But it is not enough to read simply for information. For student teachers, the first step of knowing what to read can be a daunting one, can take much time and be frustrating. We provide them with a reading list at the start to help, but they still have the responsibility to decide where to start on it, and how much to read. Similarly, when we are reading about a topic, we need some kind of baseline criterion in order to select information. Say we want to find out about how the topic of enzymes might be taught in Biology. We could start with an internet search using key terms to see if anyone has written on the relative benefits of using digital simulations. That is a way of bringing up information on the topic under scrutiny. It should leave us with more information than we had before, so now we have to narrow it down by making a selection. We need to be selective in what we read. This involves making judgements. How do we judge anything? Probing the concept of 'judgement' a bit more, we find the element of 'evaluation', with its root of value. So we select what seems to us to be of value or worthwhile. Within that choice, we then have to do some further evaluation, and here we come to the heart of criticality in reading. A set of questions is offered in the final section of this chapter which are all about evaluation.

Writing critically comes out of reading critically. Writing critically can be equated to being able to articulate our reasons for making particular decisions in the classroom. Master's students report one of the great benefits of writing the dissertation as being the confidence it gives them to explain and justify their ideas to other teachers and to senior management:

At the start of this piece of writing my area of weakness was my articulation of what I was doing and why ... I no longer perceive this to be an area of weakness.

(Caroline, MA student, 2012)

Our PGCE and MA students alike report being able to improve and vary explanations for pupils after learning how to read texts very closely, think about the ideas in them and then write about them. This is one way we make a connection between academic work and the in-the-moment demands of the classroom. This connection gives a purpose to developing a critical disposition. As our PGCE student said near the start of the chapter, we need to question, but we need to be clear about the reasons behind our questions.

Our activity must be purposeful, and for that we have to assume some value standpoint. We have to 'see' the point of something from somewhere. Our particular values, laid out in the first chapter, lead to a regard for criticality as practised by educators like Freire and outlined by Poulson and Wallace. That is, we scrutinise the claims that are made in education while respecting those who make them; we evaluate the claim, not its maker. Criticality is used constructively: '*putting your attitude of scepticism and your open-mindedness to work in attempting to achieve a worthwhile goal*' (Poulson and Wallace, 2004, p 6).

In summary, we need to have enough knowledge to engage critically with our own subject knowledge and its place in education. Reading widely and critically is essential for this. Writing critically is a way of developing the thoughts we get from reading and to take them into the classroom for the benefit of pupils. Learning to do these things takes time and practice. One of our student teachers at the end of her course expressed it as follows:

Critical thinking is not just an off-the-cuff process but requires deeper analysis. Teacher observation is invaluable experience, but unless you have the deeper knowledge of critically analysing teaching and learning, to observe with a particular objective, the process of understanding learning and teaching will only occur at a certain level.

(Heather, 2013)

Reflection

How do you keep up with the changes in your area of knowledge and expertise? What more might you do?

Reading the word, self and classroom critically

As we have seen, asking questions is fundamental to criticality. Questions are our critical tools. In supporting developing teachers to make theory and practice work together, we have found it useful to base criticality around Freire's metaphor of reading the word and reading the world (Freire, 1985). Freire's thinking is close to a big idea in philosophy and social science emerging in the 1960s and 70s; that almost anything in the world can be viewed as 'text' and can therefore be 'read' (Eley, 2013). In the context of teacher education, we are looking to read some aspects of our professional identity and our educational field as if they were texts, and to read them in a critical way.

The seven questions below have been developed using this idea of teacher identity and educational world as text, based on Poulson and Wallace's work and founded on Freire's principles of critical pedagogy. They are intended to help evaluate what we see and hear around us, as well as our own writing and practice.

Seven critical questions

1. Am I thinking actively about what I read, or see in classroom life?

In actively thinking about an issue, it is hard not to come up with some kind of product, an idea that is new to us, because we have brought some new information together for ourselves and made something from it. In writing, this could be a new sentence, one neither we, nor anyone else, has written in exactly that way. In practice, it could be a change such as the one made by Kate (not her real name), a foreign languages student teacher. Kate saw new vocabulary being presented in her first placement school using a particular kind of languages pedagogy, where new nouns were presented in isolation from any other 'joining' language. She then read papers on an alternative, where nouns are introduced already embedded in a sentence (Door, 2000; Mitchell, 2003). Kate considered the pros and cons of both approaches and put them in the context of a principle she considered worthwhile (her values) about giving learners maximum exposure to the target language. Kate then changed her own practice when introducing new vocabulary so that she included a verbal phrase on each slide with each new noun in order that learners could see how the noun was used in language they already knew. For example, *J'aime le tennis* (I love tennis). Kate was able to articulate the history of practice change, with her rationale. Her articulation of it meant she could write it down and use it in an assignment. Here critical reading, practice and writing are combined. Kate freed herself from simply having to follow what she saw around her, and was able to accelerate her own learning.

2. Am I actually taking on board what the writer or classroom practitioner is saying or am I too busy with my own ideas?

Academic reading and writing can, in our experience, be frustrating when you are grappling with the seeming intensely practical nature of classroom and school life. We want to get on and *do* things, to have our own ideas. A teacher educator needs a strong rationale for including theory in the 'doing', but also needs to model the benefits.

As a teacher in an education program, I cannot be satisfied simply with nice, theoretical elaborations regarding the ontological, political, and epistemological bases of educational practice. My theoretical explanation of such practice ought to be also a concrete and practical demonstration of what I am saying.

(Freire, 1998, p 49)

In other words, we need to '*practice what we preach*' (Hallet, 2010). But we do need, for the reasons given above, to think deeply about theories. Kate's story is one illustration of how theory, derived from practice and research, can help teachers develop. We think this comes about from exposure to new ideas; if we can appreciate a different view on matters in the world and consider it in the light of our own experience, something new can happen for us. But to get the most from a different view, we have to give ourselves time to actually see it. Using the 'view' metaphor, you arrive at the top of a hill you have never walked up before, and as you look out over the landscape laid out before you, you think about how much it reminds you of the time in the Pennines, when you were on holiday that time ... and at that moment you are paying more attention to the memory than to this view. One of Jean-Jacques Rousseau's biographers, Leo Damrosch, explains how he developed his own method of study which led him to an intimate understanding of other writers' ideas which was sometimes lacking in scholarship at the time.

Noticing that authors were in perpetual disagreement, he realised that he was in no position to adjudicate among them. 'While reading each writer, I made a rule for myself to adopt and follow all of his ideas without adding my own or anyone else's and without ever disputing with him ... I'll start by collecting a storehouse of ideas, true or false, but distinct, and wait until my head is sufficiently equipped to compare and choose among them'.

(Damrosch, 2007, p 144)

We don't have to believe that Rousseau pursued this method very strictly, or kept to it for long, but we can take the important point from the spirit of it; find out what the author is saying in her own terms first, before imposing our own view on it. In practical terms, we suggest to students that they try to read the whole text first in that spirit of curiosity, to find out what is there. There is no rush to agree or disagree. First of all, enjoy the view. Then comment on it. Critical reading can appear as if it were in opposition to reading for enjoyment, and yet to approach it in that way would seem to deny that we can get pleasure from intellectual stimulation. If we as teachers and teacher educators do not enjoy ideas, how can we hope for our classrooms and training contexts to be places where pupils take pleasure in scholarship and intellectual activity?

3. Do I understand the context of what I am reading or hearing?

Placing the words in context is a fundamental part of thinking actively when reading and listening. We think about when a text was written, who it was written for and what kind of writing it is. Is it a school or government policy document, a report on research written for stakeholders, or perhaps an idea (thinkpiece) based on the writer's own thinking and experience and meant to provoke? It is vital to know, as criticality means being able to judge something in its own terms. '*Different types of literature tend to emphasise claims to different kinds of knowledge. Each type of literature is also subject to particular limitations affecting the validity of the claims it embodies*' (Poulson and Wallace, 2004, p 19).

Context is important so we know how to judge writing and situations. Let's assume that we have already made the initial judgement that reading it is relevant to our particular purpose. That is the judgement *re* selection; knowing what to read is as much part of becoming a critical reader as the act of reading itself. Then we need to know how much weight we can give to the contents, perhaps as a general idea that we may find interesting in itself, or in its practical implications. It may have been a good idea at the time, or it may be inappropriate because things have changed. It may have been peer reviewed, as mentioned earlier, or perhaps is having a first airing. If the author makes it clear which it is, we are able to make some kind of evaluation. We can bear all that in mind when we ourselves write, or present ideas to colleagues, or try something out in the classroom in front of a student teacher.

Teacher educators tend to choose some texts for student teachers to read, especially at the start of their course. That selection has to be justified and purposeful, with a range of kinds of texts and with the intention of increasing academic literacy. Similarly, a choice has to be made of which speakers to invite for students to listen to, which teachers to ask to give input on educational issues, and which to model teaching. Students need to be able to apply their critical faculties to what speakers say and teachers do, and do not to have to accept everything they see or hear. They can then ask the next question.

4. Is the piece of writing/teaching sequence coherent? Does it make sense?

In selecting our reading, trying to understand the main idea and researching the context, we will have considered contents, but now comes the focus on the way written text or oral presentations are constructed. In this step, we clarify the claims a writer is making by looking at how each step is logically related. (Note this will not be the case necessarily in a piece of poetic writing, so again, it is vital to know what kind of text we are engaging with). We know that many of our students, both PGCE and Master's, find it very hard to construct arguments in a sequential way. We can use Dewey's consecutive thinking discussed in Chapter 2 to give a sense of the nature of internal coherence. It does seem easier for us to practice associative thinking than consequential thinking. Think of doing a brainstorm, where we write up all the ideas that come up from one topic and all contributions are accepted. Then think of writing those disparate ideas into a coherent whole. Putting ideas into a logical sequence places more demand on us than brainstorming. 'Thinking it out', as Dewey suggests (Dewey, 1933, p 7), involves thinking about a topic from all sides, but then in writing about those sides in some sense of order, building to an 'end' or conclusion. Following a skilled writer's consecutive line of thought can be instructive in terms of how to do this and you could choose anything from the further reading sections in this book to try it out.

5. How does it fit our own experience?

In criticality, we must give our own experience some status; we are not just playing with words and clever arguments, but are weighing words against reality, and our take on how reality works (our ontology). Borrowing a concept from John Searle, an American philosopher of mind and language, we want to see if the words we read or hear 'fit' with our existing knowledge of how things are. Searle calls this 'word-to-world fit' (Searle, 1983/2004, p 7). There is an academic tradition where ideas are compared with other ideas, without reference to practical experience. In Searle's account that means we are fitting word to word, comparing what two writers say. Knowing what different people are saying about educational matters is important, but we can make more of this kind of knowing for developing teachers, by comparing it constantly to the world of practice.

Searle suggests that language can be used in two ways, in an 'assertive' way and in a 'directive' way. Looking at these categories from the point of view of written text, an assertive text is one like Bourdieu's description of 'field', or Caroline's words in Chapter 2: 'My field has changed from one that was narrow, restricted not by a picket fence but chains'. In these instances, the writers make assertions, or propositions, about how the world seems to them. Searle calls this 'world-to-word direction of fit' (1983, p 7). In a directive text, the intention is to suggest, or give an order, about how something in the world should be changed. A national curriculum is an example of this kind of 'word-to-world direction of fit'.

We need to know what kind of text we are reading, as different kinds of texts require different responses. For example, when reading a prescription for curricula, there is an implicit demand to imagine how the meaning of the words could be applied in the world. Some kind of comparison is suggested, between what is and what could, or should, be.

6. Are other perspectives included?

It is important to know what kind of writing we are reading, or what kind of talk we are listening to, so that we can 'read' it in the right spirit. If it is made explicit that the purpose is to describe or report on some experience of the writer it is considered justifiable not to include other perspectives than one's own. But in a talk at a conference, or in an article in a professional journal, the convention is that the writer includes other perspectives, demonstrating that she has thought and read widely and is able to set her own work in context. So when we read critically, we must look for awareness of alternative perspectives. We can transfer that to writing because at Master's level the literature review specifically provides the space for the writer to demonstrate this awareness. In close reading of a journal article, we can learn much from the way writers present and engage with arguments which are alternative to their own.

So, once again, we can use the act of critical reading to prepare us for writing critically. Students writing at Master's level need to show they understand and can communicate someone else's ideas. In the classroom, student teachers in schools need to be open to the input they get from watching and listening to their mentor and other teachers. I am sure you can see how the critical part of reading and writing transfers to other contexts. We can listen critically to someone and ask questions. We can apply the same questions to ourselves when we speak, in presentations to colleagues, or in contributions to meetings (and we can be aware that others are listening to us using the same criteria). We think that this level of thoughtfulness is part of being a critical teacher or teacher educator with a goal of always developing our own and others' practice.

7. What are the writer's or practitioner's values? Are they explicit or implicit? How does the writer or practitioner position themselves as an educator in relation to learners?

As you can see, this is a three-part question. I have tried to simplify it, but it just doesn't seem to do the job if I do. It is a tool to tackle perhaps the hardest thing in critical reading and listening, because it involves trying to see something that is often hidden, even from the author. Some writers make their values explicit throughout their work. For example, Freire makes it clear he is writing from a political position, which is that of 'the context of democratic thought', and from a philosophical position, where humans and human society have both the potential and a duty to keep on developing. He describes this as *'human unfinishedness'* (1998, p 31). His position on teaching and learning flows from these principles and it is hard to find inconsistencies with those values in his writings regarding his particular democratic vision.

In practical terms, Freire's approach in the classroom is one where there is more dialogue than 'telling', as the learners' existing knowledge and experience is valued and built on. Heather, one of our PGCE students, wrote that criticality in the classroom was:

... in terms of teaching and learning, to be able to engage learners in meaningful dialogue which may result in learners adopting deeper knowledge and understanding of their subject and/or their process of understanding why they do something and what they can do to improve.

(Heather, 2013)

In our experience at Keele, it is usually possible in observing a teacher teach, to see what their real values are as regards their role, the role of students and the role of knowledge. However, in reading, it may not always be possible to tell what the writer's values are, or if they act in accordance with them. It is even arguable whether that matters in terms of the impact what they say can have upon us. When we write or speak, we can make a decision about whether it is appropriate to refer explicitly to our own values, as I have tried to do in this book, or whether we simply need to ensure that we can be comfortable with the tone and content of what we say, without actually formulating our position.

Of course, we can't always see our position clearly as it is so close to us. Patricia Hinchey (2010) gives example of her student teachers who, when asked why they gave homework, responded: 'What do you mean, why did I give homework? That's what teachers do!' (p 2). In giving this kind of response, we are accepting the way things are. Sometimes that is the best option. For example, it is unwise for a student teacher to openly question and then to reject the way things are done in their placement school. Firstly, such a thing would presuppose that the student understood the whole complex context of the school. Secondly, it would be to mistake the relationship that they are granted by the educational system when they are on placement. But the questions can be asked and should be asked as, when qualified, those teachers may find themselves in a position where they can thoroughly explore context and offer constructive ideas for change.

... being critical is to not just 'take' things as given facts, but to question them in order in the end to have an opinion based on thought and evidence ... not being critical makes you a playball of others, their influences, 'truths' and views of the world. If you don't mind that, I think there is no point, but if you want to be an individual, it is quite useful.

(Sophie, 2012–13)

Reflection

On a large piece of paper or using a piece of software which allows you to do a mapping exercise, map out your view of knowledge in your subject area. What do you need to know; what do your learners need to know? Then go back and put in who determines that knowledge and what justifications there are for including it in the curriculum.

Criticality is creative

As we will see in the next chapter, criticality is a creative enterprise. In the words of one of our student teachers: 'Before embarking on my PGCE journey I had no awareness of critical thinking. When challenged, I would have said ... it is about criticizing ...' Later this same student said that it was 'through being critical and observing the lesson ... that I learn, and try to think of different ways to stay creative' (Sophie, 2012–13).

IN A **NUTSHELL**

Criticality is essentially a disposition towards enquiring into how the world of educational practice works and what is said about it. Being constructively sceptical but open to what educational knowledge is, and how it came to be considered as knowledge, can be seen as creativity. Critical reading and writing are currently considered to be benchmarks for teachers in many areas of the world, and we can capitalise on that to deepen our understanding of our field. Being critical involves working out what our own views on education are and being able to express them. We practise criticality by asking the right questions at the right time and of the right issues, and always relating them to practice. If we consciously do this ourselves, we are in a position to help others do it too.

REFLECTIONS ON **CRITICAL ISSUES**

- *Criticality is a disposition to be curious about professional issues and to demand evidence from self and others as regards policy and practice.*
- *Properly practised, it provides a way to link theory to practice and practice back into theory. It involves the practitioner in wanting to become more informed, but using their own judgement on information.*
- *A similar level of criticality is now accepted in most areas of the world in higher education, and is becoming more widespread in some areas in teacher education.*
- *There are key questions which the teacher educator can demand of themselves in order to go through the process which will enable them to help others practise criticality.*

Further reading

Freire, P (1971) *Pedagogy of the Oppressed*. New York: Herder and Herder.

Freire, P (1998) *Pedagogy of Freedom*. Oxford: Rowman and Littlefield.

Poulson, L and Wallace, M (2004) *Learning to Read Critically in Teaching and Learning*. London: Sage.

Searle, J (1983/2004) *Intentionality*. Cambridge: Cambridge University Press.

- *What does creativity mean in an educational context?*
- *Why is creativity important?*
- *What does creative teaching and learning look like?*
- *What are the challenges of creativity in teacher education?*

Introduction

The previous two chapters have focused on the teacher and teacher educator as reflexive and critical. Now comes a far more problematic area of educational practice – creativity. It is clear from the title of this book and of this chapter that I think creativity should be included as part of a teacher's early development, but its inclusion raises far more challenges for teacher education than do reflexivity and criticality.

In the last chapter, a view of criticality as one of enquiry was put forward; there were questions about the way educational knowledge is talked about, both in schools and in the literature. The latter included how such knowledge is interpreted and conveyed to the practitioner through national policy, and how practitioners re-interpret knowledge to our classes. The main aim in that chapter was to suggest that the goal for the critical practitioner is to become as widely informed as possible on the central and peripheral issues of education and to keep on widening and deepening that information base and to seek out new information and relate it to practice. Chapter 2 considered how reflexivity is a means to a seamless interchange between theory (including policy) and practice, a way to practice what we preach, thus avoiding that form of intellectualism which fails to bridge the gap between rhetoric and reality.

The dispositions of reflexivity and criticality demand thought and work for both student teachers and teacher educators, but they could be said to be fairly uncontroversial and in fact complementary to most existing schooling systems. A creative disposition, however, raises fundamental challenges to certain views of schooling and certainly demands careful consideration of its nature, justification and implementation in the classroom.

I have argued that teaching reflexivity and criticality to others (student teachers or students in classrooms) means practising them ourselves. Teaching creativity requires even greater clarity of what it is we are doing and what our own position is on it, as well as the skill to actually do it.

This chapter differs from the previous two in that it lays out some issues which cannot be resolved by anyone but you, the reader. What I have tried to do is to explain the background to creativity as a recent theme in schooling, to raise some issues and possibilities in order to help you formulate your own views, and to lay out what I see as the challenges for teacher education. It may seem an impossible dream to recommend to busy professionals that they take the creativity theme slowly and enjoy it as they go. But surely creativity is something to be enjoyed and savoured, and although the doing of it may respond well to a bit of pressure, appreciating its fruits is best done in a relaxed way. Just as you would want to lead your student teachers gently towards a disposition which will help them keep developing practice, so for any teacher educator, whether relatively new to or experienced in working creatively, it is important to have time and plenty of opportunity to read and reflect on it without rushing.

In this chapter I *problematise* the term 'creativity' in education, that is, get under the surface of the notion with the aim of seeing the complexity and nuanced issues that are implied by that one word, 'creativity'.

How is creativity conceptualised in education?

In 1997, the New Labour government in Britain published a White Paper whose stated underlying purpose was to raise standards of literacy and numeracy in order to improve attainment in school (Blunkett, 1997). This was different from the previous Conservative prime minister's call for a return to basics (*The Guardian*, 1993). The Paper made it clear that we should have learned from experience that improvement in those basic skills was not going to happen without '*raising morale, motivation and self-esteem in schools*' (NACCCE, 1999, p 1). Basic skills were not so basic after all. Something more fundamental was needed, specifically the underpinning of curriculum and teaching with something which fostered the '*creativity, enterprise and scholarship of all our people*' (Blunkett, in NACCCE, 1999, p 1). The report was followed in 1999 with the title *All Our Futures*, under the chairmanship of Sir Ken Robinson, who continues to campaign for schools globally to take on creativity (HuffPost/TED, 2014). The group he oversaw was composed of a wide range of people, eminent in their field at that time, who were sympathetic to the idea of creativity – academics, actors, business people, head teachers, musicians and television executives – although any charge of lobbying for the arts specifically was firmly denied in the document; this was a cross-curricular approach. The group consulted an extensive list of organisations and individuals for its conclusions (see NACCCE, 1999, pp 234–41). There is an underlying assumption that 'creativity' is much more than students producing creative products such as paintings, poems and plays, although it may well encompass such traditional outcomes. The main points of the group's position are quoted below to illustrate this:

> » Creative learning involves '*thoughtful playfulness ... It is serious play, conjuring up, exploring and developing possibilities then critically evaluating and testing them*' (NACCCE, 1999, p 107) and '*a special flexibility in which there may be*

a conscious attempt to challenge the assumptions and preconceptions of the self – an unusual activity in which there is an active effort to unlearn in order to learn afresh' (NACCCE, 1999, p 107).

» It is *'driven by the need to find, introduce, construct or reconstruct something new. It seeks actively to expand the possibilities of any situation … learning of creative thought is not neutral; it has a bias towards the innovative'* (NACCCE, 1999, p 107).

» So, *'creative activity can itself be regarded as a form of learning particularly suited to the testing and complex conditions and which will face us all in the twenty-first century'* (NACCCE, 1999, p 107).

» And it involves *'love of learning and the desire for personal growth, realising the potential of the individual in some form of creative activity'* (NACCCE, 1999, p 109).

Between 1999 and 2010 there was considerable investment across the primary and secondary levels of education in Britain, including support for developing in-service teachers, but in 2011 after an economic crisis and a change of government the project was effectively over (CEE, 2012).

Robinson, who became an icon for creative educational practice in his YouTube appearance entitled *'Schools Kill Creativity'* (Robinson, 2007), has been consistent with his 1999 definition of creativity as *'having original ideas that have value … it's a dynamic process that often involves making new connections, crossing disciplines and using metaphors and analogies … Creativity is about fresh thinking. It doesn't have to be new to the whole of humanity … but certainly to the person whose work it is'* (Robinson, 2013). He is insistent on the non-linear nature of creativity, which does not sit well with a linear model of learning. Robinson's point has consistently been that schools in England and the United States cannot cultivate the qualities they claim they want for their young people if they insist on separating the mastery of skills and acquisition of bodies of knowledge from the cultivation of motivation to *do* the mastering and acquiring. Ironically, it was the recognition that motivation of students in our schools needed boosting in order to improve attainment that led ostensibly to the *All Our Futures* report in the first place.

I draw on the report as our starting point because it is an education policy document rather than a book about creativity and so it gives a unique insight into the tensions facing educationalists. I recommend anyone interested in the place of creativity in education to read the 1999 report, remembering that it was written at a particular time, in a particular context, with a particular agenda. In other words, it was not neutral. However, it does seem to represent a very genuine attempt to engage with the knotty problem of alternatives to standardised teaching to the standardised test and the demotivation of many pupils and teachers.

It is possible to view the report as being instrumental, being concerned with motivation merely in order to raise the attainment of entrants to the workforce for national economic benefit. In fact it opens with a mention of *'education as a vital investment in "human capital"*

(NACCCE, 1999, p 1). However, there is a deal of emphasis on its relevance for social cohesion. That was the reason for inclusion of a cultural strand, to allow those in education '*to engage positively with the growing complexity and diversity of social values and ways of life*' (NACCCE, 1999, p 6). Creativity and culture were conceptualised together like this: we need to understand and respect different cultures and values at a time when both are rapidly changing. '*The engine of cultural change is the capacity for* **creative thought and action**' (my emphasis) (NACCCE, 1999, p 7).

Post 2010 in England and Wales, national government's policy on intercultural understanding and respect for values is no longer explicit, and the role of creative thought and action, as well as any financial or structural support, has been scaled down (see Brennan, Hatchett and Lloyd, 2013). The emphasis in the new curriculum in England and Wales is now firmly on knowledge (Viner, 2013). One argument for this is that too much importance has been placed on learner-centred pedagogy, with a loss of direct-transmission teaching which has been to the detriment of knowledge acquisition (Christodoulou, 2013).

Reflection

Does creativity privilege certain techniques, such as group work, or use of games to engage students, at the expense of the teaching and learning of knowledge? Can there be a creative approach to enabling knowledge acquisition underlying almost any classroom technique? Observe a range of lessons to see the nature of the interaction between learners, activities and knowledge acquisition.

There have been several publications on creativity in the classroom since 1999 (eg Craft, 2005; Savage and Faultey, 2007). I do not wish to duplicate the ideas and information contained in those books, but draw out two of the major distinctions contained in them in an attempt to get under the surface of what creativity means in the context of teacher education.

The first distinction is that between a special kind of creativity which tends to make people famous, such as the composing of music, painting of pictures, discovery of new solutions in mathematics, or the development of new technologies, and that which is specific to individuals and more everyday. Anna Craft (2005, p 134) uses the terms 'big C' and 'little c' to capture the difference. Using criticality, we can see that what is happening here is the coining of specific language to convey an idea. The terms in themselves are meaningless without our assent to them, which should include our own understanding, from our own experience, as well as an understanding of the author's context and reasons for employing them. With a cautious acceptance of what they entail, we can then use them as cognitive tools with which to view the world and our own experience (Egan, 1997). We can use 'big C' and 'little c' as a kind of shorthand, but should be careful not to mistake the words themselves for some kind of reality. In fact we may decide that there can be an overlap. The terms do not account for the kind and amount of work required to turn what might be a good idea into a reality which may be shared with others. They can help us to find out what our own position is on this aspect of creativity.

Reflection

Can only certain kinds of people, geniuses or the specially talented, practise creativity, at special times, over long periods or in certain conditions, or can we all do it in small ways, at every moment of our lives where there is a decision point? Again, observe lessons to see the nature of small-scale decision-making and the kind of consequences those decisions seem to have on learners.

Craft (2005, pp xxiii; 41) also developed two related ideas from the *All Our Futures* report: teaching creatively and teaching *for* creativity. The former refers to the way a teacher chooses to make her own pedagogy engaging, so that students find it interesting and even inspiring, perhaps motivating them to further study. The latter labels the concept of a pedagogy which aims to support students themselves to think and act creatively. There has been discussion on the usefulness of separating the two ideas, claiming that it is an over-simplistic dichotomy which does not reflect the interrelatedness of both (Jeffrey and Craft, 2004; Savage and Faultey, 2007). What is important for our purpose in terms of teacher education and developing teachers is that we explore the ideas, both by reading what has been written and by holding it up to the daylight of actual classroom practice. We can then take informed decisions on how we may work with the ideas with student teachers.

In this book, I use 'creative practice' and 'creative practitioner' to cover what Craft calls 'teaching creatively' and 'teaching for creativity' (eg Craft, 2005, p 41).

Starting with ourselves

Resourceful, passionate, self-aware, flamboyant, solution-seeking, maverick

Do these words above describe for you in any way what it means to be creative? They are examples of the words we get when we work with students, both pre- and in-service teachers, having started by asking for their ideas of what the creative teacher looks like for them, either in words or pictures. The student-led activity is reflexive: the way we as individuals think about things will influence the way we interact with those things, which in turn will have an impact on how those things turn out both for ourselves and for any others whom we involve. So we start by unpacking our own thoughts on creativity. If we do that, we may begin to understand how our student teachers, and our students in the classroom, may react to the notion of creativity. Given the nature of 'big C' creators, can we hope to be like Mozart, Einstein or Van Gogh? Should we even want to emulate them in a single-minded commitment to the creative act? Children may be given examples of big C people, and may see themselves as quite lacking in ability to be like them. And perhaps that is the best thing. How appropriate is single-mindedness of that sort to young people who are coming to school to be exposed to a wide range of ideas and ways of doing things? Paradoxically, those of us who think of ourselves as not particularly creative can be the key to enabling others to be little-c creative, and we suggest that little c steps can be thought of as building up to big C achievements.

Developing our own robust conceptions of creativity

If we think it is of value to enable student teachers to develop creative practice from the start, then we need to understand that some may feel that they simply are not creative and therefore not in a position to teach creatively and certainly not to teach *for* creativity. If they see themselves as creative, there is a different problem, which is a potential lack of empathy with those who consider themselves to be quite ordinary, a bit dull, and certainly not in the 'flamboyant' category. Will the 'creative' student teacher automatically know how to teach *for* creativity? We need a very clear and robust conception of our own in order to be able to lead both those with little belief and confidence and those with plenty of both towards what we may conceive as creative practice.

The following two conceptualisations, openness and creativity in the present moment, may be helpful as they offer what could be called a democratic version of creativity, a version where being open and creative is simply part of being human. We can all be open and creative in a way which is to some extent independent of culture, gender and age (although it is recognised that we can never be completely independent of any of those factors). In Craft's terminology, being open and creative in the moment is definitely 'little c'.

Knowledge-rich creativity

A key 'light bulb' for me was that creativity does not come out of nothing.

(Sophie, PGCE student teacher, 2013)

If we are not open to new experiences we will have no primary material to be creative with (Dewey, 2007/1910). We need *'a full tank of knowledge-rich deliberate learning to prime the cognitive unconscious for complex, strategic acts of creativity'* (Cunliffe, 2007, p 4). It is again a bit of a paradox; we need to enrich and extend our knowledge, yet somehow hold it at bay so it doesn't stop us taking in new information (Cunliffe, 2007). We don't want just to assimilate new ideas, and bend them to suit ourselves, says Dewey. We perhaps cannot hope to be impartial or neutral, but we can be aware of our tendencies and habitual attitudes, with the intention of putting them on hold for enough time to allow some new information to enter. In other words we need to apply critical principles of reasoning to our existing store and allow ourselves to come to provisional conclusions even if they do not sit comfortably with us. Just as we evaluate the ideas in policy and literature, we need to evaluate our own pre-existing thoughts, or we may not be as open as we could be to any new topic (Dewey, 2007/1910). Our pre-conceptions, including our prior knowledge of a subject, may interfere with our receptivity to what is revealed in a new area of exploration.

Let's approach the paradox by considering how we take in information. Work on schemata in the field of reading and cognition indicates that we create our own 'maps' of the world about how things are. If a reading text or a real-life situation fails to fit with our existing cognitive map, and we don't see a need to see it, we may simply miss it (Anderson, Osborne and Tierney, 1984; Carey, 1986). These maps are spatial, in terms of where things should be, so that if things are in their normal place, with their normal qualities of colour and shape, we take no notice, but if they are in a different place, or not in their usual place, we experience some kind of surprise. A small example would be as happened to me recently, when I arrived at a school to find it had a sign board at the entrance where there had never been one before. It turned out that it had been there for years, but it had recently been repainted. I had simply failed to notice it. It was an item of information that didn't count for me (I thought) and therefore I was not open to it.

My doctoral research was on the issue of noticing in language learning. It appears that what we are accustomed to influences what we notice in the world outside ourselves. If we are aware of that possibility, we can consciously decide to focus on the new element; my recommendations in the thesis were for students to give themselves the luxury of re-reading a text, and spotting where they may have jumped to conclusions about what the words meant, and having another look to see if that was what was really meant.

Creativity as openness

So, creativity requires input from something that is not ourselves. This is part of Dewey's concept of openness (Zeichner and Liston, 1996). Although neither Dewey or Bourdieu are perhaps renowned as theorists on creativity, they both dared to look at the world in a fresh way. Their work was dependent on much knowledge, but initially, it required much observation on their part; it was not an interior, inward-looking procedure. Bourdieu (2008) refers to the '*total immersion*' (p 3) and '*attention to trivial detail*' (p 5) involved in his studies of French peasant society, without which he would not have wanted to come to his formalised models of how things in societies work. Models built on much thinking but little observation can end up preventing us from seeing the world, rather than allowing us to see more of it. Observation and analysis are '*humble obscure tasks through which the knowing subject frees himself from the grip of his unthought past*' (p 5).

Observation is a necessary, but not sufficient, condition for us to be creative; we need a rich knowledge base and some criticality. Both Bourdieu and Dewey, who were prolifically productive in terms of writing, had to think long and hard about what they saw in the world. (Bourdieu, 2008a; 2008b; Dewey, 1933; Jackson, 1998). If we allow ourselves to be open to new information, and then ask ourselves questions about it, it seems that we can scarcely fail to come up with something which is, for us at least, new (Dewey, 2007/1910, p 17). If we take that dimension of creativity as having the capacity to innovate (NACCCE,1999, p 6) then we are, all of us, intrinsically creative, that is '*little c creative*' (Craft, 2005). In the classroom context, such a stance may be crucial to the teacher and be one way out of the dilemma of '*I have to be creative but I am a very dull and ordinary soul*'. Strangely enough, it seems that if we think about ourselves as not being particularly creative, in the flamboyant, maverick, passionate sense, we may be in a better position to teach for creativity. We will understand how our students may feel, and will have been through a process to draw out the 'little c' in ourselves and on that basis can help others to do the same.

Creativity as positive and constructive use of the moment

Creativity in the classroom is frequently associated with enquiry (eg Dewey, 2007/1910; Best, 1991). Dewey's enquiry approach sprang from his observations of the intense curiosity of young children as they actively try to make sense of the world around them. It seems crazy to ignore the energy of curiosity, but Robinson, for one, is sure that schools do just that (Robinson, 2013). We can turn to a mathematician-philosopher of a similar time to Dewey for a possible way of thinking about how we as adults can use our curiosity in a creative way. If we can do that, perhaps we can have insight into how to encourage and direct the energy of young people, rather than deadening it.

Henri Bergson, a French philosopher whose initial training was in Mathematics, gives us an idea of creativity in the present moment (Bergson, 1992/1946). In a way, the present is the only time we can *be* creative, as all of us have only this moment at any one time. And it is our individual present moment, which comes after everything that has been in our past. If we are not too preoccupied, says Bergson, we can have access, directly or indirectly, to our knowledge, all we have learnt in the past. In that moment of action, we take a decision on how to act – not as we have in the past, not constrained by it, but simply limited by the store that we have and by the connections we can make with it. Then we can think something new, behave in a new way or produce something new. The decision could be described as positive, constructive and purposeful, as it is taken towards a goal that is in some way life-enhancing. It leads towards more possibilities and growth, however tiny, rather than self- or other-destroying. This is where, for us, Craft's 'big C' and 'little c' creativity come together; we can't do it all the time, as we have pressure upon us, but we can do it on an everyday basis, as it can be such a small thing; the decision to smile not scowl, to listen not contradict, to address a child in a different tone of voice, change course in an explanation as we see the class beginning to switch off, or dare to use poetry and drama as a means of pedagogy in science or mathematics.

Donald Schön has a similar notion, which he called reflection-in-action (Schön, 1983;1987). He had been intrigued by the way experts work, and observed at times a kind of fluid problem-solving, too fast for words. This he considered more valuable than the well-practised automatic skill of experts, although the value of that was not to be overlooked. But the fluid problem-solving enables the expert to meet the situation of the moment – it was the opposite of the habitual, the mechanical, although it depended on a huge skill and knowledge base. Schön calls this *'artistry'* (Schön, 1983, Chapter 2) and notes that it can happen in any area of expertise, ranging through those such as architecture, medicine and market research. It is only about the production of new solutions or ways of doing things, rather than concrete products, although it may of course lead to production of goods.

A small study carried out in 2010 with our language student teachers revealed that they really began to reflect-in-action in the second half of their course (Smith, 2010). We picked up on this and discussed it explicitly, promoting discussions which required them to consider alternative action from the very start of learning to plan lessons. The 'what happens if …' scenario was to be considered as soon as the student teacher was able, so that it became built into planning. At the start it might be as simple as asking, when planning, 'what happens if the projector and board don't work?' and 'what happens if the class don't all arrive at the same time?' It can then develop to more nuanced considerations like 'What happens if the class are too fidgety for that explanation?' or 'What do I cut out if I have to go over something again?' We consider this to be laying the foundations of creative practice in action in the classroom. Alternatives are prepared at the planning stage, where 'what happens if' is built in to the plan. If it has been planned, then it could be argued that it is not new, it is not responsive to the moment. But in our experience it is the ability to conceive of the need for alternatives which seems to mark out the creative student teacher; those who think it is unnecessary have not perhaps been in-the-moment enough to notice that lesson planning cannot be a straightforward, linear process.

Bergson's conception of our past almost bursting with options for new ways of acting has a bearing on the lesson plan itself, as each one is new (if created by the student teacher). The plan is potentially an area of intense creative activity for student teachers, where they can call on experience and knowledge from their past, including recent knowledge of a particular class and individual students (how they were last lesson) to create a new sequence, a new explanation or new resources, or to use existing ones in a new way. This is the start of teaching creatively. Teaching for creativity involves putting our store of life knowledge and subject knowledge gained from much observation, study and practice, together with our belief in the innate creativity of individual students.

Challenges of creativity for the teacher educator

I have already looked at some challenges, our own pre-conceptions and those of our student, the need for rich subject knowledge and the difficulty for all of us of being open to new perspectives. We have just touched on the place of becoming a creative practitioner. I turn now to two further issues: security in the pedagogy of creative practice, and the paradox of innovation and autonomy.

Being secure in creative pedagogy

What are the implications of developing creative practice within a system which is no longer explicitly advocating it? Teacher educators need to be aware of the responsibility of introducing the notion of creativity as an educational principle. There may be support for it from individual schools, and there may be sympathy towards it in principle from central government (Viner, 2013) but, in our experience, there may be little or no practical or theoretical input which might sustain individual teachers who wish to develop creative teaching and learning. A student teacher may have to tread very carefully in a school or department where creativity is associated with lack of core knowledge coverage and uncertainties about the kind of learner-centred techniques criticised by Christodoulou (2013). Here is yet another reason for thinking through our own 'take' on creative practice and its implementation in reality. Teachers are responsible for their students, the school and parents for the well-being of the child in their care at any one time, for their part in the safety and running of the school as an institution, for achievement in national tests and examinations.

If we encourage the kind of creative learning environment where children can '*pose questions, identify problems and issues together with the opportunity to debate and discuss their "thinking"*' (Jeffrey and Craft, 2004, p 82), we need to be secure in leading our student teachers towards the pedagogy necessary for managing exploratory learning without a lack of curriculum coverage. Using the principles of knowledge-rich creativity, openness and creativity-in-the-moment outlined above is a practical way to develop that kind of creative pedagogy, which can be sensitive to hostile environments because it does not conceptualise creativity as flamboyant or product-orientated.

The paradox of innovation and autonomy

'*The teacher needs to be the guide on the side, not the face in the space*' (Marjorie Scardino in NACCCE, 1999, p 112). How true is this? What is your position on it?

Autonomy was considered to be fundamental to the notion of creativity by the NACCCE committee: autonomy for schools, for teachers and for students. It is recognised as an essential part of '*active learning*' (Benson, 2013), but I suggest that its implementation as an integral part of teaching and learning is not a simple matter and requires the teacher to be very clear about their philosophical and ethical position on it.

First, the simple part: if our aim is to support autonomy as part of a student's creative learning (teaching *for* creativity), we need to provide an appropriate classroom environment for it to happen. This may be a consideration of space in terms of how the classroom is laid out; it may be a question of time in terms of how much is available, and might be gained from collaboration with other subjects. Such considerations are standard for primary classrooms in England (eg Arthur and Cremin, 2010, p 118) but become immediately problematic at secondary level, where much learning is anticipated as taking place at an individual level, in rows or equivalent in science and art and design contexts, and within strict time limits.

Now the complex part: autonomy is all about power and who has it (Allen, 2007; Ball, 2013). The moment we encourage an individual to have autonomy, we are suggesting that we, as teachers, cede some of the power we are normally expected to hold. The challenge is to know how authentically you can hand over this power, what limits and conditions you set upon it. If it is autonomy without creativity, it is a much easier question, as the limits can be strict, and transgression can be punishable. When that extra demand of creativity is added, strict limits and punishment become 'inauthentic' (in opposition to the authenticity suggested as fundamental to creativity in the classroom in NACCCE 1999, p 106) and inappropriate (Robinson, 2013). It is in this space, between autonomy, learning about life, learning core knowledge and fresh thinking, where deep reflection is required.

In order to assess our own basis for handing over power, we need to come back to, as in Chapter 2, our philosophy of education. What is education about? Is it about reproducing, through schooling, the existing socio-economic and cultural situation (Bourdieu and Passeron, 1990)? In the exhortations to creativity in the NACCCE report and from those such as Robinson, it is about changing those conditions – any particular nation has to change in order to survive in the 'testing and complex conditions and which will face us all in the twenty-first century'. So we need to educate differently, then, and in a sense, as adults, none of us can know what those complex conditions will be like and what skills and strengths citizens of the future will need. But the drive to creativity was seen as a way to generate fresh possibilities, including those previously unimagined: '*This process is driven by the need to find, introduce, construct or reconstruct something new. It seeks actively to expand the possibilities of any situation*' (NACCCE, 1999, p 172). So then, do we encourage children to think differently and to perhaps come up with ideas which we, as educators, had not imagined?

Reflection

Think back to your observations in the two previous reflections, on learning through games and teachers' decision-making in the moment. What elements of freedom did there seem to be for learners and teachers? Can you balance freedom with knowledge acquisition?

IN A **NUTSHELL**

The main challenge when leading others into creative teaching and learning is to think through our own position on the nature and means of achieving creativity. If we believe that creativity has a place in educational practice, we must cultivate our own disposition in regard to it.

In doing that we can consider our position, knowledge and skills regarding:

» The nature of creativity: what is it? According to whom? Who has it?

» What is the intention of any current policy with regard to creativity?

» What time and kind of space in the curriculum is there in which it can be implemented?

» What are the issues of responsibility implied if we implement it ourselves, or encourage others to do so?

» What limits to freedom do we think there should be for learners?

» How do we support developing teachers to approach creative practice?

REFLECTIONS ON **CRITICAL ISSUES**

Having read the chapter, what is your thinking on the following statements? All or any of these statements could be used as a start for discussion with student or newly qualified teachers.

• 'Where creativity has an important place in the curriculum, pupils generally have very positive attitudes to learning and enjoy coming to school' *(NCSL, 2004, p 2).*

• *Learning is linear.*

• *There should be specified principles promoting creative education within any national curriculum.*

• *Creativity is only possible with certain kinds of classroom and curriculum arrangements.*

- *Creativity and culture are related.*
- *'The engine of cultural change is the capacity for creative thought and action'* (NACCCE, 1999, p 7).

Further reading

Cunliffe, L (2007) Using Assessment in Knowledge-Rich Forms of Learning and Creativity to Nurture Self-Regulated Strategic Intelligence. [online] Available at: www.google.co.uk/url?sa=t&rct=j&q=&esrc=s&source=web&cd=1&ved=0CDUQFjAA&url=http%3A%2F%2Fcreativityconference07.org%2Fpresented_papers%2FCunliffe_Nurturing.doc&ei=g1MCUZ3JE4e00QWL1YHAAQ&usg=AFQjCNF (accessed 25 January 2013).

Jeffrey, B and Craft, A (2004) Teaching creatively and teaching for creativity: distinctions and relationships. *Educational Studies* 30(1): 77–87.

NACCCE (1999) *All Our Futures: Creativity, Culture and Education Report to the Secretary of State for Education and Employment and the Secretary of State for Culture, Media and Sport.* [online] Available at: www.sirkenrobinson.com/pdf/allourfutures.pdf (accessed 20 May 2014).

CHAPTER 5

DEVELOPING THE RESEARCHING PRACTITIONER

CRITICAL **ISSUES**

- *How does research link to the three dispositions?*
- *What kind of research can student teachers do?*
- *How could research be good for pupils, teachers and schools?*
- *What is research?*
- *What does knowledge mean in the context of research?*

Introduction

In this final chapter there is a return to all three dispositions to explore their implications in the initial and continuing development of educational practitioners. It is suggested that enquiry in the form of research is a way forward for development, whether practitioners are at the start of their preparation or whether they are at a stage where they can have responsibility for preparing and developing others. Using the dispositions to underlie research is a means to link what could seem to be a formal, theoretical activity to everyday classroom or wider school practice. Doing research on that practice is a way to feed practice back into theory, by generating original knowledge. However, the chapter is not specifically a 'how to do' of research. Instead it gives explanations and examples intended to help practitioners who may not have a background in research to understand some of its principles, and to make literature on how to do it more accessible. In addition, it is to help those who have responsibility for getting student teachers or others to research, by discussing the role of small-scale research within a school.

Reflection

Ask yourself whether your thinking is developing. What signs of it can you bring to mind? Is it visible to yourself and others in your practice? Note down specific ways in which you think your changed thinking shows in action. Return to those notes from time to time to see if the process of development is continuing.

Recapping the dispositions

Reflexivity

Practitioners seek to understand their own thinking and behaviour, and how they might impact on others, seeing themselves in the wider context in which they live and work, influenced and shaped by particular cultures and economic and political situations. They attend to acting out their own educational values, but always work to understand and respect those of others. They bear in mind that we are all human.

Criticality

Practitioners think and read as widely as possible in order to understand perspectives other than their own, and to develop confidence in their own intellectual and practical judgement. They question what they think and read, and try to discern what lies under the surface of an idea or text. They work to have deep and wide understanding of their subject, and use reading and thinking together with their classroom experience to exercise good judgements, especially in the face of changing views on what constitutes good learning, teaching and curriculum content.

Creativity

Practitioners use all their experience, knowledge and sensitivity to think about curriculum and pedagogy in new ways, being open to alternative explanations and ideas. They think through the implications of creativity for pupils, teachers and schools. They work to create their own alternative explanations and ideas, and consider what and how to teach in a way that both engages pupils in the creative act of learning and sustains their own interest in the profession.

What's the point?

The point and purpose of all the aspects of these dispositions is to enable teachers to have a flourishing and sustainable educational practice, which at the same time will benefit their pupils. Returning to them deliberately in everyday thinking allows them to become the means of guiding practice in a productive way so that it is enriched and, in turn, it enriches the educational experience of pupils. The dispositions are essentially about personal enrichment which can be enacted at any time, through observing, reflecting, reading and talking. In this kind of deliberative act, practical consciousness is developed discursively (Giddens, 1991).

Reflection

When having a conversation with a colleague, reading a book or paper about a particular teaching issue, see if you can be aware of gaining a new insight. Then see if you can deliberately use that insight in your practice.

Research for continuous development

If pedagogy is thought of as an art, then the job teachers have is not to *master* pedagogical content knowledge (Shulman, 1987, p 8), which includes how and what is taught and understanding who it is being taught to, but rather to go on *developing* it. Stenhouse puts it like this: '*Teachers must be educated to develop their art, not to master it, for the claim to mastery merely signals the abandoning of aspiration*' (1983, p 189). Learning to teach is not '*a static accomplishment*' (p 189) but an on-going activity, where we prize '*professional doubt and uncertainty*' (p 190). Stenhouse warns that pursuing certainty in terms of pedagogic practice is a false path for teachers, as it is likely to simplify teaching, learning and curriculum for a political or ideological reason. If we want security in practice, then the best thing to do is seek it in uncertainty, that is, in knowing that we can't know it all (the corollary of that is that neither can anyone else) and there is always something more to learn, and a new way to think about it.

This echoes the claim in Chapter 1; if teacher educators want to encourage these positive dispositions in their students, they themselves need to be continuously developing them (Hallet, 2010). However, some framework is required to keep practice alive and growing and research can provide just that. Throughout this book the kind of enquiry that practitioners can do at any time has been advocated, that is, critical reflection on everyday practice. All that is needed to tip this informal activity into something more formalised is to add systematicity and rigour to it. This might be by recording what was done and why, how it was done, and why the practitioner chose to do it that way. Enquiry done systematically and transparently in that way can be called research.

Stenhouse provides a definition of research which gives a sense of how to cope creatively with the kind of 'not knowing' or epistemological insecurity mentioned above when he calls it '*the controlled and organised exploitation of such uncertainty in the disciplines of knowledge*' (1983, p 189).

The context of research

In the chapters on reflexivity and criticality, the importance of understanding and being explicit about context was mentioned; that is, the time, place and relevant factors of any particular event. This might be a teacher's own context as a practitioner within a particular school, the context of the school in the area, or the political policy context in which all those things are situated. In contextualising their own reading and writing, teachers practise part of the criticality introduced in Chapter 3, that of recognising that no text or story about an event is neutral; it is always told from a particular point of view.

Context gives information which can enable us to understand an event or a text. Stephen Ball begins his book on Foucault (2013) with an account of his own journey as a researcher, his desire for certainty and for a secure academic identity. He then explains how Foucault's work freed him from his quest to be safe and his desire '*to be a "something"*' (2013, p 2). He thus gives the reader the chance to see where his writing is 'coming from', to know what he may want us to believe, and how much weight we can place on what he says. Other authors are less explicit about their intent, and so are less easy to situate in our understanding. I think there is very little difference between context helping us understand an author, and it helping us to understand why a particular student teacher might have problems in giving explanations to a class, or why the class itself may have particular difficulties in understanding them. In order to set teacher research in context, I give a brief history of its growth.

Research for learners and teachers

As mentioned in Chapter 3, at the time of writing there is a growing expectation globally that primary and secondary teachers should become critical practice experts (Aspland, 2006; Bologna, 1999; Darling-Hammond, 2005; Foley, 2012; Grant and Agosto, 2008; Guo, 2012; IITE, 2014). That means we should not simply consider the curriculum to be unproblematic, nor should we take for granted suggested ways of teaching it. Instead we need, just like our pupils, to be thinking actively about our subject knowledge, what it should consist of, and how it can be acquired. In addition, as teachers and teacher educators, we clearly also have to think about how we enable others to acquire it.

Enquiry-led methods have existed for learners for a long time, tending to appear in what are sometimes labelled 'progressive' educational settings (for a history and critique of progressive education, see Howlett, 2013). Names such as Rousseau, Froebel, Montessori, Steiner and Dewey are associated with children learning for themselves through exploration. The government-sponsored Plowden Report of 1967 explicitly recommended a discovery approach (Plowden, 1967; Gillard, 2011) and the STEM Pupil Research Briefs sought to promote investigation as a learning tool in science, technology and mathematics between 2000 and 2009 (STEM, 2014a). Progressive education has been attacked for a perceived tendency to privilege process over solid facts, or as having *'temporary relevance over a permanent body of knowledge'* (Gove, 2008, in Howlett, 2013) but an exploration of the STEM website or their *Catalyst* (STEM, 2014b) journal for teachers will show how enquiry for *pupils* is still valued by professional subject organisations. This has relevance for the role of classroom practitioners in terms of being able to help pupils to research.

Teacher research has a more recent history and seems to begin to emerge in Britain in the late 1960s, for example with the Schools' Council (government-funded) Humanities Curriculum Project. This project aimed to develop a cross-curricular approach in English, history, geography, RE and sociology, which encouraged enquiry for pupils and critical reflection on curriculum and classroom practice by teachers (Stenhouse, 1983: Hopkins, 2008).

A culture of classroom research gradually spread. During the 1990s and early 2000s, there were government bursaries in England and Wales for small-scale practitioner research, which allowed classroom teachers enough funding for resources to undertake their own project, either in their own or in other schools (eg Teacher Learning Academy, 2008). By 2010, a full-scale Master's programme, the Master's in Teaching and Learning, had been introduced. This was an initiative by the Labour government of the time which gave access for newly qualified teachers and Heads of Department to a free Master's-level course, run for in-service teachers in their own schools, with input from consortia of higher education institutes, whose role was also to prepare mentors in school to support their own MTL students. No formal national evaluation of the MTL has yet been published but those who finished the MTL reported gains in insight and motivation, for example this PE teacher, who reported to me that doing it:

gave me confidence and support for when I needed it most during my NQT year and early development of teaching. I would certainly advocate the importance of professional reflection which I believe the course promoted and supported.

(Darren, 2014)

Central funding for the MTL ceased in March 2011. However, the British Educational Research Association (BERA), which can be seen as the *'UK's leading learned society in the field of educational research'* (BPS, 2013), has produced a key report for the case of practitioner research. The authors use extensive national and global evidence to argue that teachers who are *'research literate and have opportunities for engagement in research and enquiry'* (BERA-RSA, 2014, p 5) are good for pupils and good for schools. In addition, currently in England the guidance for Teaching Schools includes a criterion for staff development through research (Teaching Schools, 2014) and there is now funding for Master's work on special educational needs (gov.uk, 2014). Wales has introduced the Master's in Educational Practice (wales.gov.uk, 2013). In Scotland, thanks to the Donaldson Review, the policy framework now exists for implementing structures to enable and support teacher research (Donaldson, 2011). A long-standing commitment in Northern Ireland to the value of teacher enquiry has not yet been translated into action, but the BERA-RSA report (2014) contains detailed recommendations for its implementation.

Research is good for pupils, schools and teachers

It is not clear, even now, whether all schools understand, value and support teacher research, despite the growing body of evidence-based literature (Handscomb and MacBeath, 2003; Hargreaves, 2007; Hopkins, 2008; Sharp, 2006; Wilkins, 2011; BERA-RSA, 2014). However, as Hopkins (2008) and Wilkins (2011) point out, teachers researching their own classrooms as part of their professional development should be seen as a fundamental aspect of school improvement. They are in no doubt that a national focus on key skills, such as literacy and numeracy, can certainly lead to increased standards, but the ceiling for this is soon reached if the individual classroom teacher is not directly involved in the school's efforts to achieve it. If teachers raise their level of subject knowledge (in terms of depth and width of understanding) and their ability to make good professional judgements, then the capacity of the profession to respond to national and local priorities increases. Without that individual professional development, it does not. Some head teachers do recognise the benefit of a research culture to pupils, staff and the system more widely:

Every adult should have regular opportunities to carry out research, extending professional knowledge, based on what happens in their own classrooms and those of colleagues ....

This process is central to enriching the intellectual life of the profession, leading to renewed excitement within the classroom.

(Tarleton, 2005, pp 89, 92)

Even if there is no such process, student teachers researching in their placement schools can sometimes be a catalyst for change, as in the following case study of a Keele student for whom I was the general studies tutor.

Case study: Andrew

As a student mathematics teacher at Keele, Andrew had to research an aspect of his placement school and give it as a presentation to his tutors in the school and to his Keele general studies tutor. He chose to look at the school's current reward system, which was a commercial one, requiring investment by the school. Andrew used his own observations and pupil questionnaires to make an initial exploration of how pupils regarded the system, to which he added his own perspectives as a student teacher. At the presentation, it was clear to us all that Andrew had revealed some new insights into the working of the system. School staff saw that his work needed to be shared and developed in a systematic way across the school and then could potentially have an influence on whether the school would continue to use it, but in a more effective way, or whether they would move to another system. This small step in practitioner exploration could turn out to provide a basis for significant whole-school change and may be indicative of the benefits which school-based teacher education will have to offer.

Research and autonomy

The issue of autonomy in the classroom was specifically discussed in Chapter 4 in the context of creativity. Practitioner autonomy has been an implicit theme throughout the book. In Chapter 2, I drew attention to Dewey (1933) and Bourdieu (2008) considering how to develop independent judgement by understanding how thinking works and how it interacts with a person's practical experience and their professional role. In Chapter 3, I referred to Freire's writing of the role of the teacher in the cycle of domination and how, through becoming aware of it, and of their own role in it, they can break it and transform the world (1978). In the same chapter, mention was made of Poulson and Wallace (2004) discussing the move from a culture of acceptance of authority in academic practice towards an expectation of a critical stance, which means teachers must develop autonomy in the way they deal with new information on pedagogy and curriculum. The question of how much autonomy a teacher is prepared to cede to pupils in the interests of creativity was raised in Chapter 4.

Classroom-based research provides a means to autonomy as it puts the practitioner into the role of expert, rather than into the passive role of deliverer of a particular pedagogy and curriculum content. It is an appropriate kind of research for furthering pedagogy and some aspects of curriculum change (Hopkins, 2008; Selwood and Twining, 2005; Stenhouse,

1983). The nature of any research done is responsive to what practitioners want to find out and why they want to find it out. The classroom teachers are ideally placed to observe what is really going on in their classes and to think about the knowledge base that may underlie any evidence they find in regard to it. To quote Dewey again, there is the opportunity to give '(a)ctive, persistent and careful consideration of any belief or supposed form of knowledge in the light of the grounds that support it and the further conclusions to which it tends' (1933, p 9). Through this process, it is possible that the practitioner will find new solutions for what may be a common problem.

Being in such a privileged position (in the very context which is to be researched) I think gives a teacher ownership and control of the knowledge which she generates, that is, epistemological autonomy.

In summary, research provides a reason and a way to develop practice, and 'develop' in this instance means to change. If practice is changed simply because an external agency demands it, without initiative and critical engagement from teachers, there is a danger of de-skilling (Stenhouse, 1983). We cannot allow classroom practice to remain the same, because if it does, it becomes mechanical (Stenhouse, 1983; Hopkins, 2008). Times change, ways of looking at life change. It seems good to avoid running to keep up with changing times and new generations of young people, and better to go for a more gentle and continuous growth that allows us to be flexible and to innovate when we detect a need to do so.

Teacher research is of value to pupils, teachers and the school as a whole. It has the potential to enhance the quality of the teaching and learning from the point of view of pupils. For teachers, it has the potential to open new perspectives on old problems or on issues that are intriguing to the individual, that are, as Stenhouse puts it 'rooted in acutely felt curiosity' (1983, p 185). In that last sense, researching is very much part of the teacher's creativity and can be seen as 'creative thought and action' (NACCCE, 1999, p 7).

What is research?

Thinking critically can be described as questioning, evaluating and reflecting on some situation or proposition (Chapter 3). Researching includes those actions, and includes finding out something new. This something may in fact be a different way of looking at the world, which entails understanding a phenomenon in a new way (Lowe, 2007; Stringer, 2004). This could be new for the individual teacher, or for someone else, or for both as in the case study above.

Reading the literature critically for information and ideas was discussed in depth in Chapter 3, but in this chapter the way of doing research, and the thinking behind that way, is brought into focus. I include here a discussion of the terminology, as that is one of the things that our PGCE, MA and doctoral students have found most confusing. I give some initial definitions here. Their purpose is to help you construct a basis of understanding, so that you can come to choose the definitions which appeal to you. Note that the ones here are all referenced. If you read a term, or use it yourself, you need to ensure you are clear where it comes from.

The overall thinking behind a research project and the eventual form it takes is known as the '*research design*' (Blaxter, Hughes and Tight, 2004, p 62). Research in education takes different forms, and what is carried out is very much dependent on purpose, that is, what the researcher wants to find out and why she or he want to find it out. The design has to relate to the purpose. But in addition, the researcher has to be aware of what they understand the *nature* of the topic of research to be. In the case study above, Andrew, even though a mathematician, did not assume that the way a reward system in a school operated should be measured statistically. His interest was in how pupils and staff thought about the system and how they used it. His perspective or view of the world was '*interpretive*' (Denzin and Lincoln, 2003, p 34) or '*constructivist*' (Robson, 2002, p 27). Had he decided that what was important was to measure use by number of times the system was used within a certain period and balance that against financial input, his perspective could be termed '*positivist*' (Lowe, 2007, p 9; Robson, 2002, p 16). This term is used here in the context of the field of social science (note that 'positivist' in some social science references can be pejorative).

Some writers simply use the words 'qualitative' and 'quantitative' to describe the world-view (see Punch, 2005, p 27 for a useful explanation), but those who try to promote a more nuanced understanding use the word 'paradigm' to define the underlying attitude towards the focus of research and the kind of knowledge with which it deals (Denzin and Lincoln, 2003). Understanding the term 'paradigm' allows an understanding of one of the three basic concepts of research in the social sciences, which is where educational research can be said to sit (Hammersley, 2007, p x). Those concepts, with a brief explanation, are:

» ontology: how we believe the world to be; our perspective or world-view on the nature of the focus of our research;

» epistemology: how we know the world is like that; the kind of knowledge we are seeking, and perhaps generating in our research;

» axiology: the ethics we adopt in researching.

Our ontology will determine both what we think is possible to research, and the overall way we research it. Our epistemology will determine the kind of knowledge we think we can discover or generate, and through that, the way we find out. That way, and the way we then go on to analyse what we find out, and the implications we draw from that analysis, can be termed '*methodology*' (Clough and Nutbrown, 2007). Our students have found it useful to think of methodology as our overarching epistemology, stemming from the paradigm, and then research methods become the means used to actually collect information, or data, for example questionnaires, interviews, observations or personal reflections.

It is important to understand that the knowledge claimed to result from research is always dependent on the ontology, epistemology and axiology of the researcher, as well as the more mundane question of who the research was funded by and with what intentions, as only then can we decide how much weight to give it, and how relevant it is for our situation. This kind of understanding is what could be called a critical understanding of the research process and the knowledge it may produce. As Stenhouse puts it: '*Knowledge ... is falsified when it is presented as the results of research detached from an understanding of the research process which is the warrant for these results*' (1983, p 180).

Axiology is not developed further in this chapter; each school or place of research will have its own rules about what is permissible in researching, and those can be taken together with the reflexive disposition defined in Chapter 1 and at the start of this chapter, specifically regarding how practitioners *attend to acting out their own educational values, but always work to understand and respect those of others. They bear in mind that we are all human*' (the reflexive disposition).

Three examples of educational research are given below to show the link between ontology and epistemology as well as to give an idea of what research possibilities a group or an individual may have. The third example is the most relevant for teacher researchers, so the discussion after it is correspondingly longer.

Large-scale research

Some educational research is on a very large scale, for example, that carried out by the Programme for International Student Assessment (PISA). The stated aim of PISA is to provide information to allow '*countries and economies to compare best practices and to further develop their own improvements, ones appropriate for their school systems*' (PISA, 2013, p 1). The research is funded by the departments of education in the participating countries, and is contracted out to private companies (PISA, 2014). It is carried out on huge populations; 65 countries took part in the 2012 survey to assess '*the extent to which 15-year-old students have acquired key knowledge and skills that are essential for full participation in modern societies*' (PISA, 2013, p 1) and involved about 510,000 school pupils in a 2-hour-long test and a 30-minute-long questionnaire. This kind of research is about education, but it is not 'practitioner research', which is the kind of research that we would encourage our student teachers to do. It combines a view of the world that considers that achievement can be measured statistically with a realisation that in understanding achievement, the way individuals within large groups think needs to be taken into account. It could be said that the methodology used and the knowledge that is claimed to arise must be carefully scrutinised, as achievement and attitude will be inevitably affected by the widely differing social and educational contexts of all of the participants.

Medium-scale research

Medium-scale educational research is illustrated by that done by two US university-based researchers. Liang and Dixon (2009) were commissioned by the Centre for Research and Pedagogy in Singapore to begin to explore the nature of the possible impact of teachers' beliefs on educational change. The researchers did not try to prove anything about impact, but took the necessary first step in the exploration by finding out what teachers' beliefs are. This was done by interviewing 75 teachers individually and in small groups (focus groups) and then separating what they said into categories. The ontology here seems to be that policy implementation is not a straightforward thing and is inextricably linked to the individual's beliefs. There may, however, be an underlying assumption that beliefs can be changed and moulded to suit policy imposition. The knowledge generated must be regarded critically in order to detect the particular ontological bias.

Proving things in education research is very problematic, due to the complexity of the area; think back to the map of your own practice you made in Chapter 2. Hopkins describes '*the myriad of contextual variables operating on schools and classrooms (eg community culture, teacher personality, school ethos, socio-economic background)*' (2008, p 42). 'Proving' anything requires very clear isolation of variables, which is very difficult for classroom teachers. In both the studies cited above, the emphasis was on gathering data rather than proving a hypothesis. In educational research that first step can very often be simply finding out what *is*. This may be on the basis of a hunch (or informal hypothesis) but the desire to go straight into proving the hunch has to be resisted if the research is going to stand up to any kind of public scrutiny (Poulson and Wallace, 2004). This is where we start with our student teachers. Whatever topic they choose to explore, they look at through the lens of their own practice first. In doing this, they are practising reflexivity.

Case study: small-scale, individual research

This kind of education research does not require any extra funding, so, as the researcher is not beholden to anyone for money, she can be autonomous in what she looks for and what she finds out. The ontology is reflexive, in that it assumes a close relationship between researcher and focus, both set in a particular context. The epistemological assumption is that it is possible to find out about 'what is' in teaching, through systematic reflection and input from other informed sources, such as another teacher. Although in the example below the main empirical work was carried out in a classroom, such research can be done in any area of the school, for example, a study of behaviour of pupils or perhaps, staff, around school, at parents' evenings, or in the canteen. The example below is the kind of exploration which you may have done on your own pre-service course and is shared courtesy of a student, 'Jane' (not her real name), from our MFL teacher education course (2013).

Jane considered that she was not differentiating sufficiently for all her pupils. She reached that conclusion from her own lesson evaluations and from feedback from observers. Her research aim was to explore her own use of differentiation and that of others, with the longer-term intention of improving her teaching. She started researching by reading around two topics:

1. what had been written about differentiation, specifically in a secondary classroom context;

2. what had been written about how to research such a focus (methodology).

Jane's reading on differentiation enabled her to problematise the use of differentiation, both as a term used in policy and discussion, and in practice. 'Problematise' is used here in Foucault's terms of '*how and why certain things (behaviour, phenomena, processes) become a problem*' (Foucault, 1983, in Ball, 2013, p 26). Her reading on methodology led her to choose action research as a justifiable way of designing the project. Briefly, action research has been taken to be an appropriate methodology for groups or individuals finding out what is going on in a practice situation with a view to improvement (Greenwood and Levin, 2007; Hopkins, 2008; Selwood and Twining, 2005). In action research finding out something new (knowledge production) is not the major focus, but it has to happen as a preliminary to any improvement. Jane needed to find out what she did in differentiating, as a first step to any improvement.

Research and knowledge

This first step is highly reflexive and critical, as it is about a teacher's own thinking and action, illuminated by a '*wider body of knowledge*' (Selwood and Twining, 2005, p 2) from the evaluation of literature and discussion with other professionals.

Unlike in the educational policy topics explored in the first two examples above, where work is conducted under special conditions by those particularly trained in educational research and dependent on external funding, small-scale individual work can be done by a student teacher. Andrew's and Jane's cases show that looking at an issue in a very local environment of one school can lead to original knowledge creation. It is carried out by a teacher as s/he works in the everyday world of the classroom (Selwood and Twining, 2005). The findings may not be generalisable, but can help the teacher know where to go next in his or her own practice. However limited the findings may be in terms of applicability, they have been generated by the action of the researcher. If they are shared with others, either within school or in a publication such as a professional journal, they can serve as a source of ideas to the wider world of school and national and international publishing (for example the case studies in Wallace and Poulson (2004) and Hopkins (2008)).

Research for knowledge generation

Going through the process of research gives the teacher a first-hand insight into how theory can help with practice, and how practice can feed back into theory. Having to choose a way of finding out about, or exploring a particular classroom issue, gives insight into how knowledge is generated. Knowing how to choose a focus for research and an appropriate way to research (methodology) gives the teachers autonomy when they want to be active agents in their own development and to be able to have their own discursively conscious praxis.

The theory-practice-theory cycle

Having started with '*a state of doubt, hesitation, perplexity*' (Dewey, 1933, p 12) in regard to differentiation, reading the literature gave Jane an indication that a range of perspectives was possible. Jane found that that there were several ways of looking at differentiation, which might be contradictory or might simply emphasise different aspects. She saw that writers could disagree on what differentiation means in terms of which was the best way of applying it. From holding practice in her own and others' classrooms up to the light of the perspectives, she discovered that individuals could take one definition and apply it in different ways. This went some way in explaining why teachers in her placement school seemed to have a range of ways of putting the Ofsted definition that her school used into practice. The definition: *'the matching of work to the differing capabilities of individuals or groups of pupils in order to extend their learning (goodschoolsguide.co.uk)'* was loose enough to give leeway for different approaches in the classroom, but Jane, at that stage in her development, wanted more prescription and was unable to find a consistent message from her mentor and other teachers. Kryiacou's (1998, p 43) definition, where differentiation 'involves adapting the way work is set and assessed in order to meet the need of a range of abilities within the same class', appealed to both Jane's ethics of inclusion and her understanding of learning. *'Fundamentally I believe this would ensure that all pupils were able to access the lesson content in a way, and at a level appropriate to them, which is likely to aid progress'* (Jane, 2013). Here she matched an idea to everyday teaching and learning.

Jane saw that she herself and other teachers would tend to take a particular approach, perhaps without being aware of it. For her as a student, the lack of awareness, or simple *'practical consciousness'* (Giddens, 1991), led to lack of clarity in how she should approach differentiating. By carrying out her research, she was able to bring her own beliefs and actions to Giddens's discursive consciousness. This meant she could explain them to someone else and be in a position to change them when she found more convincing evidence of a better way. In this way, Jane was using ideas in the literature to show her what was going on in her and others' practice.

Based on her more informed and sophisticated understanding of differentiation, Jane collected data on her own lesson planning, her means of assessment, observations from other teachers and from her pupils' evaluations. Her findings were that:

- » there was scope for different interpretations of the concept across one school;
- » she and other teachers could be muddled and unable to articulate how and why they were differentiating;
- » pupils who choose their own level of differentiation can hold themselves back.

Jane, in the creative act of putting some factors together and coming up with something new, had generated knowledge that was genuinely new to the school and to herself. She hoped to be able to use this knowledge in her practice from then on. She could have gone on to disseminate what she had found, by putting it into an appropriate format for a school professional development presentation, or for her professional journal, which encourages submissions from beginning teachers.

IN A **NUTSHELL**

Teacher educators need to understand the reasons for doing research. They need to be able to guide student teachers to carry out an appropriate kind of research in their initial teacher education. The best way to understand in order to lead the learning of others is to try out the activity yourself. Educational practitioners within a school do not necessarily have to carry out research on classroom teaching; it could be done on any aspect of practice, for example it could be an exploration of some of the issues involved in providing school-based initial teacher education. Being able to focus on one particular element of practice, observe it, read, think and write about it, can deepen understanding, and improve that practice. The back-and-forth of looking, thinking and then feeding back into practice makes a virtuous cycle of practice-theory-practice and can lead to new knowledge creation.

REFLECTIONS ON **CRITICAL ISSUES**

* *Carrying out some kind of research, however small in scale, is a creative activity which involves reflexive awareness of personal practice, and a critical stance towards both that practice and to what is said in policy and the wider literature.*
* *Classroom or practitioner research, that is, research that looks at issues through the lens of personal practice, is appropriate for beginning teachers, as well as those who are more experienced.*
* *Because research harnesses what seems to be an innate curiosity, it tends to keep teachers interested in their own practice and hence keeps that practice alive.*
* *Even small-scale research can generate a new insight into a pedagogical issue. That insight may not be world-changing, but it is unique and can be seen as new knowledge.*

Further reading

Denzin, N and Lincoln, Y (2003) *The Landscape of Qualitative Research: Theories and Issues.* Thousand Oaks: Sage. The introduction to this book gives a sophisticated interpretation of the emergence of the interpretive paradigms in social science research.

Hargreaves, D (2007) Teaching as a Research-Based Profession: Possibilities and Prospects, in Hammersley, M (ed) (2007) *Educational Research and Evidence-Based Practice.* Los Angeles: Sage.

Hopkins, D (2008) *A Teacher's Guide to Classroom Research* (4th edition). Maidenhead: Open University Press. A good general guide to the history, rationale, and practice of carrying out classroom research.

This book has been about how important it is for teacher educators to understand themselves and their context in order to build a flourishing practice. It has proposed that such an understanding can be built by cultivating the dispositions of reflexivity, criticality and creativity, within a culture of informal and formal practitioner research. A flourishing practice has been defined as one which keeps its practitioner interested and has an enriching effect for teachers, and student teachers, as well as on pupils and school.

Teachers who have responsibility for educating beginning teachers may well be expert teachers. In his study of expert classteachers (2012), Tony Eaude gives a description of the process whereby a novice teacher moves towards expertise, where they make that transition:

from a dependence on external rules and guidelines to a reliance on tacit knowledge, accumulating case knowledge to decide on what matters most … this involves an increasing level of flexibility and fluidity, based on prediction of likely responses and intuition, but with the ability to be more analytic when necessary … it calls for moving from acting deliberately and consciously towards relying more on intuition.

(Eaude, 2012, pp 5–6)

It is likely that you recognise that description, and that you have spent much time and work on developing your expertise. All that investment will have been well worth the expenditure in terms of your pedagogy and the resultant benefits for your classes. But taking on the role of teacher educator requires understanding how you got to where you are now and being able to model it and discuss it with others. In the terms which have been used to talk about this understanding in the book, a teacher educator needs to understand what it means to be reflexive, critical and creative, and how and why it might be useful to combine those dispositions in informal or formal research.

Our part-time MA students, who are all practising teachers, have two years in which to complete the work. They have said one of the things they have valued most about doing a Master's is the time and space they have had to make in order to think about what they do every day. Most British postgraduate initial teacher education courses are ten months long. There is much to fit in. Student teachers are expected to learn the practicalities of the classroom, as well as learning about and keeping up with the changes and demands of education policy. Developing the dispositions is not an extra add-on, which takes up more time, but a foundation for progress and continuous development. Dispositions cannot be made to happen in a specified period of time; they have to be allowed to grow in their own time. The job of the teacher educator, therefore, is to set up the conditions for that growth and sow the seed, so that the techniques of practical classroom management are acquired in the context of the bigger creative and critical picture. You cannot force anyone to develop a disposition; you can only lead by example and open up the 'space of possibles' (Bourdieu, 2004, pp 29, 100).

REFERENCES

Alexander, F M (1985) *Use of the Self.* London: Methuen.

Alexander, R J (ed) (2010) *Children, Their World, Their Education – Final Report and Recommendations for the Cambridge Primary Review.* Abingdon: Routledge.

Allen, A (2007) *The Politics of Our Selves: Power, Autonomy, and Gender in Contemporary Critical Theory.* New York: Columbia University Press.

Anderson, R, Osborne, J and Tierney, R (1984) *Basal Reader and Content Texts.* Hillsdale, New Jersey: Lawrence Erlbaum.

Aronowitz, S (1993) in McLaren, P and Leonard, P (eds), *Paulo Freire: A Critical Encounter.* London: Routledge, pp. 8–23.

Arthur, J and Cremin, T (2010) *Learning to Teach in the Primary School.* London: Routledge.

Ashby, P, Hobson, A J, Tracey, L, Malderez, A, Tomlinson, P, Roper, T, Chambers, G and Healy, J (2008) *Beginner Teachers' Experiences of Initial Teacher Preparation, Induction and Early Professional Development: A Review of Literature.* Nottingham: Department for Education and Skills (DfES).

Aspland, T (2006) Changing Patterns of Teacher Education in Australia. *Education Research and Perspectives,* 33(2): 140–63.

Baiasu, S (2011) *Kant and Sartre: Rediscovering Critical Ethics.* London: Palgrave Macmillan.

Ball, S (2012) *Global Education Inc.: New Policy Networks and the Neo-Liberal Imaginary.* London: Routledge.

Ball, S (2013) *Foucault, Power and Education.* London: Routledge.

Barnett, R (1997) *Higher Education: A Critical Business.* Maidenhead: Open University Press /SRHE.

BERA-RSA (2014) *Research and the Teaching Profession: Building the Capacity for a Self-Improving Education System.* [online] Available at: www.bera.ac.uk/wp-content/uploads/2013/12/BERA-RSA-Research-Teaching-Profession-FULL-REPORT-for-web.pdf (accessed 26 June 2014).

Best, D (1991) Creativity: Education in the Spirit of Enquiry. *British Journal of Educational Studies,* 39(3):260–78.

Blaxter, L, Hughes, C and Tight, M (2004) *How to Research.* Maidenhead: Open University Press.

Blunkett, D (1997) *Excellence in Schools: Government White Paper.* London: HMSO.

Bologna process (1999) [online] Available at: www.ond.vlaanderen.be/hogeronderwijs/bologna/documents/MDC/BOLOGNA_DECLARATION1.pdf (accessed 14 April 2014).

Bourdieu, P (2008) *Sketch for a Self- Analysis.* Chicago: University of Chicago Press.

Bourdieu, P and Passeron, J C (1990) *Reproduction in Education, Society and Culture.* London: Sage.

BPS (British Psychological Society) (2013) [online] Available at: www.bps.org.uk/bpslegacy/cp?frmAction=d etails&paperID=1258&RegionID=4&iYear=0&open= (accessed 1 July 2014).

Brennan, J, Hatchett, D and Lloyd, K (2013) Pathways: Managing and Implementing the National Curriculum 2014. [online] Available at: www.curriculumsupport.co.uk/ (accessed 9 March 2014).

Bruner, J (1969) After Dewey, What?, in Archambault, R (ed) *Dewey on Education: Appraisals.* New York: Random House, pp 211–28.

Carey, S (1986) Cognitive Science and Science Education. *American Psychologist,* 4(10): 1123–30.

Cassell, D (2014) Teachers' Perceptions of Assessment for Learning. Keele University. (Unpublished EdD thesis).

CEE (2012). [online] Available at: www.creative-partnerships.com/ (accessed 9 March 2014).

Christodoulou, D (2013) *The Seven Myths About Education*. London: Civitas.

Clough, P and Nutbrown, C (2007) *A Student's Guide to Methodology: Justifying Enquiry* (2nd edition). London: Sage.

Connell, A and Edwards, A (2014) *A Practical Guide to Learning and Teaching Computing and ICT in the Secondary School*. London: Routledge.

Craft, A (2005) *Creativity in Schools: Tensions and Dilemmas*. London: Routledge.

Cruikshank, M (ed) (1981) *30 Years of Education at Keele*. Keele: Keele Department of Education.

Cunliffe, L (2007) Using Assessment in Knowledge-Rich Forms of Learning and Creativity to Nurture Self-Regulated Strategic Intelligence. [online] Available at: www.google.co.uk/url?sa=t&rct=j&q=&esrc=s&source=web&cd=1&ved=0CDUQFjAA&url=http%3A%2F%2Fcreativityconference07.org%2Fpresented_papers%2FCunliffe_Nurturing.doc&ei=g1MCUZ3JE4e00QWL1YHAAQ&usg=AFQjCNF (accessed 25 January 2013).

Damrosch, L (2007) *Jean-Jacques Rousseau: Restless Genius*. Boston: Houghton-Mifflin.

Darling-Hammond, L (2006) Constructing 21st Century Teacher Education. *Journal of Teacher Education*, 7: 1–15.

Darling-Hammond, L, Bransford, J, LePage, P, Hammerness, K and Duffy, H (2005) *Preparing Teachers for a Changing World: What Teachers Should Learn and Be Able to Do*. San Francisco: Jossey-Bass.

Darren (2014) MTL student, 2011–13.

DES (2011) The School Curriculum: Aims, Values and Purposes. [online] Available at: www.education.gov.uk/schools/teachingandlearning/curriculum/b00199676/aims-values-and-purposes/values (accessed 25 November 2013).

DES (2013) *Teachers' Standards*. London: Crown copyright.

Denzin, N and Lincoln, Y (2003) *The Landscape of Qualitative Research: Theories and Issues*. Thousand Oaks: Sage.

Dewey, J (2007/1910) *How We Think*. Stilwell: Digireads.

Dewey, J (1933) *How We Think*. Boston: Heath.

Dewey, J (1938/1997) *Experience and Education*. New York: Touchstone.

Dickson, B (2011) Beginning Teachers as Enquirers: M-Level Work in Initial Teacher Education. *European Journal of Teacher Education*, 34(3): 259–76.

Dixon, M and Liang, R (2009) *Teachers' Espoused Beliefs for Centre for Research in Pedagogy and Practice*, NIE (Centre for Research in Pedagogy and Practice): Singapore.

Donaldson, G (2011) *Teaching Scotland's Future: Report of a Review of Teacher Education in Scotland*. The Scottish Government.

Door, V (1998) *Contrasting approaches to the teaching of foreign languages in Germany and England, with special reference to selected textbooks*. Unpublished MPhil thesis, University of Newcastle upon Tyne.

Door, V (2000) *Teaching Writing in a Foreign Language*. London: TTA.

Door, V (2006) *Attention, engagement and support in Year 9 FL reading*. Unpublished PhD thesis, University of Bath.

Eaude, T (2012) *How do Expert Primary Classteachers Really Work? A Critical Guide for Teachers, Headteachers and Teacher Educators*. Northwich, UK: Critical Publishing.

Egan, K (1997) *The Educated Mind*. Chicago: Chicago University Press.

Eley, G (2013) Is All the World a Text?, in Spiegel, G (ed) *Practising History: New Directions in Historical Writing after the Linguistic Turn*. London: Taylor & Francis, pp 35–61.

Foley, J A (2012) The Struggle for Critical Teacher Education: How Accreditation Practices Privilege Efficiency over Criticality and Compliance over Negotiation. *Critical Education*, 4(3). [online] Available at: http://ojs. library.ubc.ca/index.php/criticaled/article/view/182433 (accessed 19 May 2014).

Freire, P (1971) *Pedagogy of the Oppressed*. New York: Herder and Herder.

Freire, P (1985) Making Meaning, Learning Language. *Language Arts*, 62(1): 15–21.

Freire, P (1998) *Pedagogy of Freedom*. Oxford: Rowman and Littlefield.

Freire, P (2006) *Pedagogy of Hope*. London: Continuum.

Gardner, J (ed) *Assessment and Learning*. London: Sage.

Giddens, A (1991) *Modernity and Self-Identity: Self and Society in the Late Modern Age*. Cambridge: Polity.

Gillard D (2011) Education in England: A Brief History [online] Available at: www.educationengland.org.uk/ history (accessed 1 May 2014).

Giroux, H (1988) *Teachers as Intellectuals: Towards a Critical Pedagogy of Learning*. Westport: Bergin and Garvey.

gov.uk (2014) [online] Available at: www.gov.uk/government/publications/national-award-for-sen-co-ordination-learning-outcomes (accessed 1 July 2014).

Gove, M (2013) *The Guardian*, 9 May, in Howlett, J (ed) *Progressive Education: A Critical Introduction*. London: Bloomsbury.

Grant, C A and Agosto, V (2008) Teacher Capacity and Social Justice in Teacher Education. *Educational Leadership and Policy Studies Faculty Publications*. Paper 5. [online] Available at: http://scholarcommons. usf.edu/els_facpub/5 (accessed 19 May 2014).

Greenwood, D and Levin, M (2007) *Introduction to Action Research: Social Research for Social Change*. Thousand Oaks: Sage.

Grenfell, M (1998) *Training Teachers in Practice*. Cleveland: Multilingual Matters.

Guo, L (2012) From Laoshi to Partners in Learning: Pedagogic Conversations across Cultures in an International Classroom. *Canadian Journal of Education* 35(3): 164–79.

Hallet, F (2010) Do We Practice What We Preach? An Examination of the Pedagogical Beliefs of Teacher Educators. *Teaching in Higher Education*, 17(5): 589–605.

Hammersley, M (2007) *Educational Research and Evidence-Based Practice*. Los Angeles: Sage.

Hargreaves, A (1995) *Curriculum and Assessment Reform*. Buckingham: Open University Press.

Hargreaves, D (2007) Teaching as a Research-Based Profession: Possibilities and Prospects, in Hammersley, M (ed) (2007) *Educational Research and Evidence Based Practice*. Los Angeles: Sage.

Hargreaves, D (2013) Professional Capital: Transforming Teaching in Every School. [online] Available at: www.youtube.com/watch?v=PpFTisH82Dk (accessed 15 April 2014).

Hickman, L and Alexander, T (eds) (1998) *The Essential Dewey, Vol. 1*. Bloomington: Indiana University Press.

Higgins, C (2010) The Virtues of Vocation: From Moral Professionalism to Practical Ethics. *Journal of Philosophy of Education*, 44: 2–3.

Hinchey, P (2010) *Finding Freedom in the Classroom: An Introduction to Critical Theory*. New York: Peter Lang.

Holland, M, Evans, A and Hawksley, F (2011) International Perspectives on the Theory-Practice Divide in Secondary Initial Teacher Education. Paper delivered at the Annual Meeting of the Association of Teacher Educators in Europe, University of Latvia. [online] Available at: www.shu.ac.uk/_assets/pdf/ceir-ATEE2011-theory-pract-MikeHolland.pdf (accessed 14 April 2014).

Hopkins, D (2008) *A Teacher's Guide to Classroom Research* (4th edition). Maidenhead: Open University Press.

Howlett, J (2013) *Progressive Education: A Critical Introduction*. London: Bloomsbury.

Huff Post/TED Weekends (2014) Do Schools Kill Creativity? [online] Available at: www.huffingtonpost.com/sir-ken-robinson/do-schools-kill-creativity (accessed 6 March 2014).

Indian Institute of Teacher Education (2014) [online] Available at: www.iite.ac.in/ (accessed 8 May 2014).

James, M (2006) Assessment, Teaching and Theories of Learning, in Gardner, J (ed) *Assessment and Learning*. London: Sage, pp 47–60.

James, M and Pedder, D (2006) Beyond Method: Assessment and Learning Practices and Values. *The Curriculum Journal* 17(2):109–38.

Jane (2013) MFL student teacher. Keele University PGCE. Keele University.

Jeffrey, B and Craft, A (2004) Teaching Creatively and Teaching for Creativity: Distinctions and Relationships. *Educational Studies* 30(1): 77–87.

John, P (2000) Awareness and Intuition: How Student Teachers Read Their Own Lessons, in Atkinson, T and Claxton, G (eds) *The Intuitive Practitioner – on the Value of Not Always Knowing What One Is Doing*. Buckingham: Open University Press, pp 84–106.

Johnston, B, Ford, P, Myles, F and Mitchell, R (2011) *Developing Student Criticality in Higher Education*. London: Continuum.

Keele (2014) MFL Student Teacher Evaluation. Keele University (unpublished).

Labaree, D F (2008) *An Uneasy Relationship: The History of Teacher Education in the University*, in Cochran-Smith, M, Feiman Nemser, S and McIntyre, J (eds) *Handbook of Research on Teacher Education: Enduring Issues in Changing Contexts* (3rd edition). Washington, DC: Association of Teacher Educators, pp 290–306.

Lawes, S (2003) What, When, Why and How: Theory and Foreign Language Teaching. *Language Learning Journal*, Winter, 28: 22–28.

Liang, R and Dixon, M (2011) Singapore Teachers' Espoused Beliefs: Links to Practice. NIE Research Brief Series. [online] Available at: http://hdl.handle.net/10497/4439 (accessed 8 May 2014).

Lloyd, G (2011) personal communication.

Lowe, M (2007) *Beginning Research: A Guide for Foundation Degree Students*. Oxford: Routledge.

McIntyre, D (1995) Theory, Theorizing and Reflection in Initial Teacher Education, in Calderhead, J and Gates, P (eds) *Conceptualising Reflection in Teacher Development*. London: Falmer, pp 39–52.

McIntyre, D (2009) The Difficulties of Inclusive Pedagogy for Initial Teacher Education and Some Thoughts on the Way Forward. *Teaching and Teacher Education*, 25: 602–8.

McLaren, P and Leonard, P (1993) *Paulo Freire: a Critical Encounter*. London: Routledge.

McPeck, J E (1981) *Critical Thinking and Education*. Oxford: Martin Robinson.

Martin, J (2002) *The Education of John Dewey: A Biography*. New York: Columbia University Press.

Marshal, B and Drummond, M (2006) How Teachers Engage with Assessment for Learning: Lessons from the Classroom. *Research Papers in Education* 21(2):133–49.

Menter, I (2013) Teacher Education Research: Past, Present and Future, in *The Future of Teacher Education and of Teacher Education Research*. London: BERA/Bamboo House Publishing.

Menter, I, Hulme, M, Elliot, D, and Lewin, J (2010) *Literature Review on Teacher Education in the 21st Century*. Edinburgh: The Scottish Government.

Miller, D, Averis, D, Door, V and Glover, D (2004) From Technology to Professional Development: How Can the Use of an IAW Enhance the Nature of Teaching and Learning in Secondary Mathematics and Modern Languages? *Report to BECTA.*

Mitchell, R (2003) Rethinking the Concept of Progression in the National Curriculum for Modern Foreign Languages: A Research Perspective. *Language Learning Journal* 27: 15–23.

Moon, J (2004) *A Handbook of Reflective and Experiential Learning: Theory and Practice*. Oxford: RoutledgeFalmer.

Moore, A (2007) Beyond Reflection: Contingency, Idiosyncrasy and Reflexivity in Initial Teacher Education, in Hammersley, M (ed) *Educational Research and Evidence-Based Practice*. Los Angeles: Sage, pp 121–38.

NACCCE (1999) *All Our Futures: Creativity, Culture and Education Report to the Secretary of State for Education and Employment and the Secretary of State for Culture, Media and Sport.* [online] Available at: http://sirkenrobinson.com/pdf/allourfutures.pdf (accessed 5 March 2014).

NCSL (2004) *Developing Creativity for Learning in the Primary School: A Practical Guide for School Leaders.* London: NCSL.

OECD (2013) Ready to Learn: Students' Engagement, Drive and Self-beliefs. Vol III: Ch1.

Ozga, J (2008) Governing Knowledge Through Data in England: From Regulation to Self-evaluation. *European Educational Research Journal* 7 (3): 261–72.

PISA (2012) [online] Available at: www.oecd.org/pisa/keyfindings/pisa-2012-results-overview.pdf (accessed 2 May 2014).

PISA (2013) [online] Available at: www.oecd.org/general/frequentlyaskedquestionsfaq.htm (accessed 3 May 2014).

Plowden, B (1967) *Children and their Primary Schools*. Central Advisory Council for Education. London: HMSO.

Potts, C (2013) personal communication.

Poulson, L and Wallace, M (2004) *Learning to Read Critically in Teaching and Learning*. London: Sage.

Punch, K (2005) *Introduction to Social Research: Quantitative and Qualitative Approaches*. London: Sage.

Robinson, K (2007) *Schools Kill Creativity*. YouTube, uploaded 7 January 2007. [online] Available at: www.youtube.com/watch?v=iG9CE55wbtY (accessed 5 March 2014).

Robinson, K (2013) To encourage creativity, Mr Gove, you must first understand what it is. *The Guardian*, Comment is Free, 17 May, 2013 (accessed 5 March 2014).

Robson, C (2002) *Real World Research* (2nd edition). Malden, MA: Blackwell.

Savage, J and Faultley, M (2007) *Creativity in Secondary Education*. London: Learning Matters.

Scannell, D (1999) *Report to the American Council on Education Presidents' Task Force on Teacher Education.* [online] Available at: www.umd.umich.edu/casl/natsci/faculty/zitzewitz/curie/TeacherPrep/74.pdf. (accessed 12 December 2012).

Schön, D (1983/2011) *The Reflective Practitioner*. London: Ashgate.

Schön, D (1987) *Educating the Reflective Practitioner: Towards a New Design for Teaching and Learning in the Professions*. San Francisco: Jossey-Bass.

Schön, D (1992) The Theory of Inquiry: Dewey's Legacy to Education. *Curriculum Inquiry* 22(2):119–39.

Searle, J (1983) *Intentionality*. Cambridge: Cambridge University Press.

Selwood, I and Twining, P (2005) *Action Research*. [online] Available at: www.becta.org.uk. (accessed 19 May 2014).

Shulman, L (1987) Knowledge and Teaching: Foundations of the New Reform. *Harvard Educational Review*, 57 (1): 1–21.

Smith, A K (2010) Unpublished MA. Keele University.

STEM (2014a) [online] Available at: www.nationalstemcentre.org.uk/elibrary/collection/1161/pupil-research-briefs. (accessed 19 May 2014).

STEM (2014b) *Catalyst: Secondary Science Review*. London: Gatsby Science Enhancement Programme.

Stenhouse, J (1983) *Authority, Education and Emancipation*. London: Heinemann.

Stenhouse, L (1975) *An Introduction to Curriculum Research and Development*. London: Heinemann.

Stringer, E (2004) *Action Research in Education*. Columbus, Ohio: Pearson.

Tarleton, J (2005) Teachers as Researchers: The Changing Role of Teachers' Education. *Education Review*, 18(2): 89–95.

Teacher Learning Academy (2008) *Becoming a Teacher Learning Academy Support Partner*. GTC & Cambridge Education.

Teaching Schools (2014) [online] Available at: https://www.gov.uk/teaching-schools-a-guide-for-potential-applicants#research-and-development (accessed 19 May 2014).

The Guardian (1993) Major goes back to the old values. [online] Available at: www.theguardian.com/politics/1993/oct/09/conservatives.past (accessed 6 March 2014).

Torrance, H and Pryor, J (2001) Developing Formative Assessment in the Classroom: Using Action Research to Explore and Modify Theory. University of Sussex. *British Educational Research Journal*, 27(5): 615–31.

Troman, G (1996) Models of the 'Good' Teacher: Defining and Re-Defining Teacher Quality, in Woods, P (ed) *Contemporary Issues in Teaching and Learning*. London: Routledge, pp 20–37.

Tryggvason, M T (2009) Why is Finnish Teacher Education Successful? Some Goals Finnish Teacher Educators Have for Their Teaching. *European Journal of Teacher Education*, 32(4): 369–82.

Twing, J, Boyle, B and Charles, M (2010) Integrated Assessment Systems for Improved Learning. 36th Annual Conference of the International Association of Educational Assessment (IAEA), Bangkok, Thailand. Iowa City: Pearson Assessment and Information.

Zeichner, K and Liston, D (2014) *Reflective Teaching and the Social Conditions of Schooling*. New York: Routledge.

INDEX